ONE HUNDRED YEARS OF PEACE

THE MACMILLAN COMPANY
NEW YORK · BOSTON · CHICAGO · DALLAS
ATLANTA · SAN FRANCISCO

MACMILLAN & CO., Limited
LONDON · BOMBAY · CALCUTTA
MELBOURNE

THE MACMILLAN CO. OF CANADA, Ltd.
TORONTO

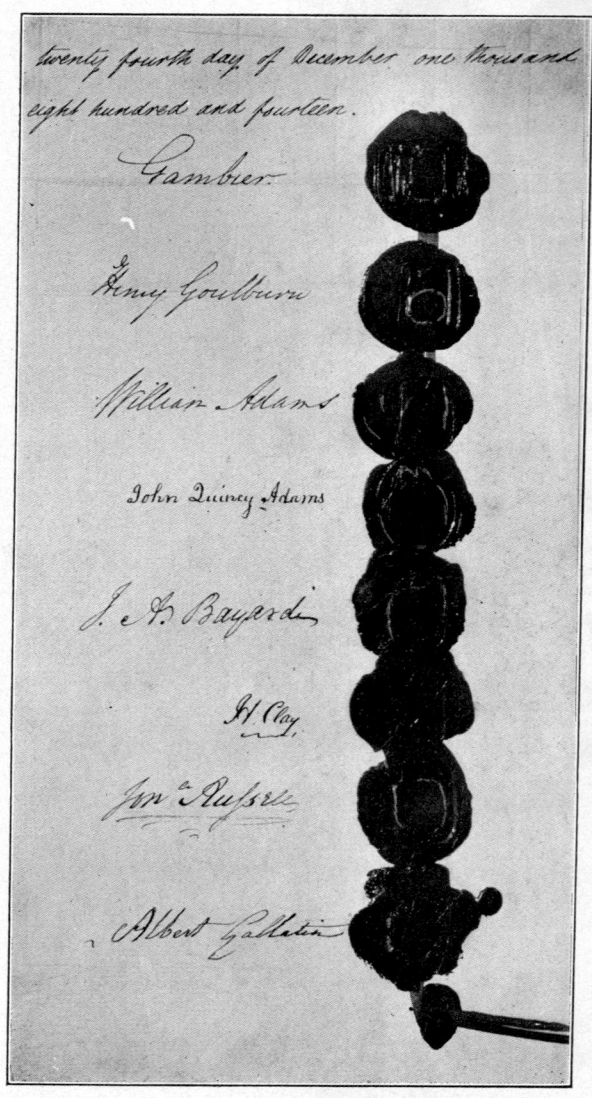

FACSIMILE OF THE SIGNATURES TO THE TREATY OF GHENT

ONE HUNDRED YEARS
OF PEACE

BY

HENRY CABOT LODGE

WITH ILLUSTRATIONS

New York
THE MACMILLAN COMPANY
1913

All rights reserved

COPYRIGHT, 1912,
BY THE OUTLOOK COMPANY.

COPYRIGHT, 1913,
BY THE MACMILLAN COMPANY.

Set up and electrotyped. Published September, 1913.

Norwood Press
J. S. Cushing Co. — Berwick & Smith Co.
Norwood, Mass., U.S.A.

PREFATORY NOTE

This sketch of the relations between the United States and Great Britain during the century which has elapsed since the War of 1812 appeared first in the "Outlook." To the publishers of the "Outlook" I wish to express my thanks for their kind permission to reprint here the two original articles revised, corrected, and much enlarged.

LIST OF ILLUSTRATIONS

FACSIMILE OF THE SIGNATURES TO THE TREATY OF
GHENT . . . . *Frontispiece*

                                                                    FACING PAGE

"WHAT? YOU YOUNG YANKEE-NOODLE, STRIKE YOUR OWN
FATHER?" 24
JOHN QUINCY ADAMS 36
ROBERT SOUTHEY, CHARLES DICKENS, AND SIDNEY SMITH 44
JAMES BRYCE, WILLIAM MAKEPEACE THACKERAY, AND
WASHINGTON IRVING 58
WOODCUTTER'S CABIN ON THE MISSISSIPPI . . . 62
THE SOLEMNITY OF JUSTICE 64
DANIEL WEBSTER 74
LORD ASHBURTON 78
REAR-ADMIRAL CHARLES WILKES, U. S. N. . . . 90
LORD PALMERSTON 96
ABRAHAM LINCOLN 100
LORD JOHN RUSSELL 108
CHARLES FRANCIS ADAMS 110
"THE LAND OF LIBERTY" 120
THE CHAMPION MASHER OF THE UNIVERSE . . . 130

ONE HUNDRED YEARS OF PEACE

THE last war between Great Britain and the United States began in June, 1812. There has been no war between the two countries since the treaty of Ghent was signed on Christmas eve in 1814. Strictly speaking, the absence of war constitutes peace, and therefore we may describe these hundred years just passed as a century of peace between the United States and Great Britain. But in the larger and better sense of the word it must be confessed that the relations between the two countries during that period have been at times anything but peaceful, and often far from friendly. Indeed, there have been some perilous moments when war has seemed very imminent. To describe this period therefore as one of unbroken good will merely because there was no actual fighting would be wholly misleading. If a review, however brief, of the relations between Great Britain and the United States since 1812 is to possess any value, it can only be through showing how, by slow steps, with many interruptions and much bitterness on both sides, we have nevertheless finally attained to the genuine friendship in which all sensible men of both countries rejoice to-day. This fortunate condition has been reached only after many years of storm and stress, which it seems to posterity, always blessed with that unerring wisdom which comes after the event, might have been easily avoided.

To understand the present situation aright, to comprehend the meaning and effects of the war of 1812 and of the ninety-eight years of peace which have followed its conclusion, it is necessary to begin with the separation of the two countries by the Treaty of Paris in 1782, when the connection between England and the United States ceased to be that of mother country and colonies and became the more distant relation which exists between two independent nations. Just now there appears to be a tendency among Englishmen to regard that separation of the eighteenth century as a small matter, especially so far as their own country is concerned, a view which, however comfortable, is hardly sustained by history, and we may well pause a moment at the outset to consider just what the war resulting in the treaties of Paris meant, for on that decisive event rests ultimately all that has since come to pass.

As an illustration of the attitude of mind to which I have referred, let me take the recent case of a well-known writer and very popular novelist. Some years ago Mr. H. G. Wells came to this country, and on his return to England, like many of his countrymen, he wrote a book about the United States. Unlike many of his countrymen, however, he wrote a very pleasant and friendly book, enlivened by some characteristic remarks in favor of socialism and of converting the Niagara Falls into horsepower. He made, however, one comment which struck me at the time, and which, I think, has been made since by others of his countrymen. This comment was in connection with his visit to Boston, as I remember, and criticised us good-naturedly for the extreme care with which we marked all spots connected with the Revolution, and for the apparent importance which we attached to that event. Mr. Wells, unlike Sir George Trevelyan, the most brilliant of living English historians, seemed to think that this American feeling about the Revolution which resulted in the independence of the United States was provincial, if not parochial. In view of the sound system of British education, which has a great deal to say about English victories, great and small, and is curiously reticent as to English defeats, it is perhaps not surprising that the importance attached to the incidents of the American Revolution in this country should surprise the average traveller from Great Britain. But, putting aside the partiality which Americans feel toward the Revolution, owing to the fact that they were victorious, and the lack of interest with which the British regard it, possibly because they were defeated, it is perhaps not amiss to point out that the war for American independence really was an event of high importance, and was so considered then, as it has been ever since, by dispassionate persons.

The revolt of the American Colonies in 1776 agitated the world of that day far beyond the parish limits of the United States. It divided parties and overthrew Ministries in England. It involved France and Spain in war with Great Britain, and created the armed neutrality of the northern Powers, events which are rarely caused by trifling or provincial struggles. But the American Revolution had results even more momentous than these. It broke the British Empire for the first, and, so far, for the only time. It took from England her greatest and most valuable possession. With the American Colonies she lost a population equal to about a fifth of the inhabitants of Great Britain at that period, as well as the ownership of the best part of a great continent. The independence of the Colonies was the foundation of the United States, and, whether one approves of the United States or not, there can be no question, I think, that they constitute to-day a large and important fact in the existing world. It was an Englishman, I believe, who said that, after all, England's most considerable achievement was the United States. Finally, and this is something which I feel it would hardly be possible to describe as parochial, modern democracy began with the American Revolution. Carlyle, who had more imagination as well as more humor than the average British commentator, either upon America or upon things in general, turns aside from a letter of Friedrich to D'Alembert which happened to be dated December 16, 1773, in order to give an account, a quite inimitable account, of the Boston Tea Party which occurred on that day. He did so because, to use his own words: "The case is well known and still memorable to mankind." It did not seem to him parochial, but on the contrary an event charged with meaning. With his penetrating and wide ranging glance, at past and future alike, Carlyle had already in one oft quoted sentence set forth what the American Revolution really meant when he wrote the history of that greater Revolution which came to pass a few years later on the other side of the English Channel. Here is what he says: "Borne over the Atlantic, to the closing ear of Louis, King by the Grace of God, what sounds are these; muffled, ominous, new in our centuries? Boston Harbor is black with unexpected Tea; behold a Pennsylvania Congress gather; and ere long, on Bunker Hill, *Democracy* announcing, in rifle volleys death-winged, under Star Banner, to the tune of Yankee-doodle-do, that she is born and, whirlwind-like, will envelop the whole world!"

Another great writer of that generation,

a friend of Carlyle, read the same prophecy in the revolt of the Colonies. With the insight of the poet, Emerson declared that the shot which the embattled farmers fired at Concord Bridge was heard " round the world," which, although expressed in verse, told the exact truth. At that bridge, in that little New England village, the first drum-beat of democracy broke upon the troubled air, and there the march began. The same drum-beat was heard soon afterwards in France, where several things happened which no one probably would regard as provincial, and which caused some stir at the time. Looking over the world to-day, it may be fairly said that no greater event could be commemorated than the first uprising of democracy which later swept over the Governments of the nineteenth century, and which is still pressing onward, crossing even now into the confines of Asia.

Yet, very characteristically, this American Revolution, which Mr. Wells smiles at gently as a little provincial incident, but which seems not to have been without its effect on the history of civilized man, turned on a question of law. That two great branches of the same people, speaking the same language, holding the same beliefs, and cherishing the same institutions, should go to war about a question of legal right in the imposition of taxes is indeed very typical of the race and breed. It is also one reason why the war of the Revolution, as a whole, was sullied by few acts of cruelty or ferocity, for, as Macaulay pointed out long ago, the character of a civil war is very largely determined by the amount of oppression which one side has suffered at the hands of the other. The government of the English colonies in America had been, on the whole, easy and liberal. Sir Robert Walpole, with his favorite motto of "Quieta non movere," with his wise indifference which allowed the dust to gather upon American despatches, and the elder Pitt, who had the faculty of arousing the enthusiasm of the colonists by

minds, and through the passions of fear and anger seized public attention with such an absorbing and relentless grasp that, naturally, no room was left for thought concerning three millions of English speaking people who had just set up a national government on the other side of the Atlantic. But it is strange that English ministers, statesmen charged with the responsibility of government in a time crowded with perils of every kind, should not have paid some attention to the United States. They were involved in a desperate war with France. Their success at sea had been brilliant, but their military failures had been little short of appalling. They were pouring out millions of pounds to pay for coalitions which one after the other went to pieces in defeat. Their subsidies were almost as completely wasted as the huge sums of money which went to the Chouans of Brittany, to the wretched following of the Comte d'Artois in London, or to the conspirators who were trying to assassinate the First Consul in

Paris. Their allies on the Continent were breaking down as the century ended, and isolation stared them in the face. One would have imagined that under such circumstances they would have looked in every corner of the globe for new friends and new sources of strength. In the United States were three millions of people, active, enterprising, pushing their vessels into every sea. These people were very largely of their own race and despite the recent war were still bound to them not only by community of language and of political belief but by the still stronger ties of long existing habits of trade, of commercial intercourse, and of thought and manners. It is true that they grudgingly drove a hard bargain with the United States in the Jay treaty. But that was all. They were content to avoid war with their former colonies, and then they turned their backs to them, even when the policy of France was forcing the Americans into their arms. It seems a

people of whom such things could be written deserved, in that great crisis of western civilization, both examination and consideration.

But there were other facts of public notoriety not concealed in the books of travellers which must also have been known to the British ministers, but which went by them apparently unheeded. They knew that the American states, shaken and broken by seven years of civil war, after five years of a weak central government, ever growing more impotent and imbecile, had come together and formed a Federal constitution. It was a constitution of an unusual character. There was nothing like it just then extant among men. A century later a great English statesman and prime minister was to speak of it as the most remarkable instrument of government ever struck off by a single body of men at one time, and Mr. Gladstone was confirmed in this view by Lord Acton, who wrote in his " History of Freedom ":

"American independence was the beginning of a new era, not merely as a revival of the Revolution, but because no other revolution ever proceeded from so slight a cause or was ever conducted with so much moderation. The European monarchies supported it. The greatest statesmen in England averred that it was just. It established a pure democracy, but it was democracy in its highest perfection, armed and vigilant, less against aristocracy and monarchy than against its own weakness and excess. Whilst England was admired for the safeguards with which, in the course of many centuries, it had fortified liberty against the power of the crown, America appeared still more worthy of admiration for the safeguards which, in the deliberations of a single memorable year, it had set up against the power of its own sovereign people. It resembled no other known democracy, for it respected freedom, authority, and law. It resembled no other constitution, for it was contained in half a dozen intelligible

might easily have made her former colonies her close friends and allies. This policy indeed was so obvious that it is hard to understand why even English ministers failed to adopt it. Jefferson, with all his eulogy of France and denunciation of England for political purposes, was more than ready to unite with her against Napoleon if England would only have allowed him to do so, but after the death of the younger Pitt and the dissolution of the Ministry of "All the Talents," the English Government fell once more into the hands of very inferior men. Ministers of the caliber of Perceval, Castlereagh, and Lord Liverpool, united with extreme Tories like Lord Eldon, whose ability was crippled by their blind prejudices, were utterly unable to see the value of friendship with the United States and preferred to treat their former colonists with a comfortable contempt. The one very clever man not in opposition in those days was Canning, and he did more than any one else, perhaps, by his unfortunate attitude to drive the United

States away from England. It was he who said that the navy of the United States consisted of "a few fir frigates with a bit of bunting at the top." For the sake of this not very humorous alliteration he paid rather heavily in the loss of a good many English frigates at a later day. Disraeli says in "Sybil" that from the death of the younger Pitt to 1825 "the political history of England is a history of great events and little men," a description of the period as terse as it was truthful, if we except the Duke of Wellington. The combination was not beneficial to England and was unfortunate for her relations with the United States.

It is not pleasant to Americans to recall the years which preceded our second war with England. There was no indignity, no humiliation, no outrage, that England on the one side and Napoleon on the other did not inflict upon the United States. Our Government submitted and yielded and made sacrifices which it is now difficult to contemplate with calmness, until at last

have suffered in the war, however much her pride might have been wounded by the destruction of the Capitol at Washington, the real victory was with the Americans. They had fought, and they had gained what they fought for. They sacrificed nothing — not an inch of territory — by so doing. The only losses suffered by the United States were in men and money, and by those losses we had put an end forever to the humiliating treatment which had been meted out to us during the first decade of the century. As the years passed by, all this became apparent, and it is now perfectly plain that the war of 1812 achieved the result for which it was fought, by establishing the position of the United States as an independent nation and restoring the national self-respect. Although the treaty of Ghent did not show it, we have but to look behind the curtain which the hand of time has drawn aside in order to learn that the men of that day in England recognized what had hap-

"WHAT? YOU YOUNG YANKEE-NOODLE, STRIKE YOUR OWN FATHER?"

pened, although they might not admit it to themselves, much less to the public. They confessed the truth in many ways, none the less clearly because the confession was indirect.

Take, for example, this letter from Mr. James, the naval historian, to Mr. Canning:

Mr. W. James to Mr. Canning

"Perry Vale, Near Sydenham, Kent: Jany. 9, 1827.

"The menacing tone of the American President's message is now the prevailing topic of conversation, more especially among the mercantile men in whose company I daily travel to and from town. One says 'We had better cede a point or two rather than go to War with the United States.' 'Yes,' says another, 'for we shall get nothing but hard knocks there.' 'True,' adds a third, 'and what is worse than all, our seamen are half afraid to meet the Americans at sea.' Unfortunately this depression of feeling, this cowed spirit, prevails very generally over the community, even among persons well informed on other subjects, and who, were a British seaman to be named with a Frenchman or Spaniard, would scoff at the comparison."[1]

The words of Mr James show the effect upon the public mind in England of the American naval victories, which so profoundly interested Napoleon. They penetrated so deeply that they actually reached the intelligence of the Liverpools and the Castlereaghs. Even they felt the meaning to England's prestige as a naval power of losing eleven out of thirteen single ship actions and two flotilla engagements on the Great Lakes. Their alarm can be measured by the honors they conferred on Captain Broke, who commanded the *Shannon* when she defeated the *Chesapeake* — higher honors than Nelson received for his brilliant service in the battle of Cape St. Vincent. Nor was this all. Despite their contempt

---

[1] "Canning Correspondence." Edited by E. J. Stapleton. Vol. II, p. 340.

for the Americans and their loud assertions of satisfaction with their successes, as the war drew to its close the ministers became so uneasy that they proposed to send Wellington to America to command their armies on the very scene of the victories which they so loudly proclaimed. The Duke's letters in regard to this proposal are most instructive, and reveal the real results of the war, for Wellington was never the victim of illusions. He had in high degree the great faculty of looking facts in the face.

On the 9th of November, 1814, he wrote from Paris to Lord Liverpool as follows:

"I have already told you and Lord Bathurst that I feel no objection to going to America, though I don't promise to myself much success there. I believe there are troops enough there for the defence of Canada forever, and even for the accomplishment of any reasonable offensive plan that could be formed from the Canadian frontier. I am quite sure that all the

American armies of which I have ever read would not beat out of a field of battle the troops that went from Bordeaux last summer, if common precautions and care were taken of them.

"That which appears to me to be wanting in America is not a General, or General officers and troops, but a naval superiority on the Lakes. Till that superiority is acquired, it is impossible, according to my notion, to maintain an army in such a situation as to keep the enemy out of the whole frontier, much less to make any conquest from the enemy, which, with those superior means, might, with reasonable hopes of success, be undertaken. I may be wrong in this opinion, but I think the whole history of the war proves its truth; and I suspect that you will find that Prevost will justify his misfortunes, which, by the by, I am quite certain are not what the Americans represented them to be, by stating that the navy were defeated, and even if he had taken Fort

Mason he must have retired. The question is, whether we can acquire this naval superiority on the Lakes. If we can't, I shall do you but little good in America; and I shall go there only to prove the truth of Prevost's defence, and to sign a peace which might as well be signed now. There will always, however, remain this advantage, that the confidence which I have acquired will reconcile both the army and people in England to terms of which they would not now approve.

"In regard to your present negotiations, I confess that I think you have no right from the state of the war to demand any concession of territory from America. Considering everything, it is my opinion that the war has been a most successful one, and highly honorable to the British arms; but from particular circumstances, such as the want of the naval superiority on the Lakes, you have not been able to carry it into the enemy's territory, notwithstanding your military success, and now undoubted military superiority, and have not even cleared your own territory of the enemy on the point of attack. You cannot, then, on any principle of equality in negotiation, claim a cession of territory excepting in exchange for other advantages which you have in your power.

"I put out of the question the possession taken by Sir John Sherbrooke between the Penobscot and Passamaquoddy Bay. It is evidently only temporary, and till a larger force will drive away the few companies he has left there; and an officer might as well claim the sovereignty of the ground on which his piquets stand, or over which his patrols pass.

"Then if this reasoning be true, why stipulate for the *uti possidetis?* You can get no territory; indeed the state of your military operations, however creditable, does not entitle you to demand any; and you only afford the Americans a popular and creditable ground which, I believe, their

Government are looking for, not to break off the negotiations, but to avoid to make peace. If you had territory, as I hope you soon will have New Orleans, I should prefer to insist upon the cession of that province as a separate article than upon the *uti possidetis* as a principle of negotiation.

And again, on November 18, 1814, he wrote to Lord Liverpool:

" I have already told you that I have no objection to going to America, and I will go whenever I may be ordered. But does it not occur to your Lordship that, by appointing me to go to America at this moment, you give ground for belief all over Europe that your affairs there are in a much worse situation than they really are? And will not my nomination at this moment be a triumph to the Americans and their friends here and elsewhere? It will give satisfaction, and that only momentary, in England; and it may have the effect of raising hopes and expectations there which, we know, cannot be realized."

Despite the "military successes," Wellington did not think that England could make any demand for territory or compensation, which shows that the "successes" had been as barren as they were trivial. The invincible troops from Bordeaux were badly beaten by Jackson, and Pakenham, one of Wellington's favorite generals, was killed, so that he did not capture New Orleans, as the Duke had anticipated.

The result was a treaty of peace that on its face only brought peace, which the Duke evidently thought was all England could expect. The pity of it all was that there need not have been any war between England and the United States in 1812, if England had only seen fit to make the United States a friend instead of a foe. But England did not so will, and the war at least taught her that the United States could no longer be bullied and outraged with impunity. Thus the war of 1812 brought, after all, a peace worth having, and laid the foundations for that larger peace which has lasted for a hundred years. During that time, through many vicissitudes, the relations of the two countries have so improved that we are now warranted in believing, what all reflecting men earnestly hope, that another war between England and the United States has become an impossibility.

These larger results of the war, so plainly to be seen now, were not of course immediately apparent. The old attitude was still too fixed, the old habits still too strong, to be abandoned in a moment. We made a brief treaty of commerce and navigation with England in June, 1815, six months after the conclusion of the treaty of Ghent, but this second treaty disposed of none of the outstanding questions as to which the treaty of Ghent had been silent, and some of these thus passed over were of a nature which imperatively required settlement. A British officer, unconscious apparently that a war had been fought, even undertook to search some of our vessels upon the Great Lakes, a little eccentricity which was not repeated.

Despite the agreement of the Ghent treaty, England held on to Astoria and the posts in the extreme Northwest, and, what was still worse, she also attempted to take the ground that our fishing rights, determined by the treaty of 1783, had been extinguished by the war. Acting on this opinion, British cruisers seized American fishing vessels, and the condition of affairs on the coasts of Nova Scotia, Canada, and Newfoundland became serious in the extreme. Mr. Adams, then Minister of the United States in London, brought these questions to the attention of Lord Castlereagh, urging upon him the necessity of further treaties to settle these disputes, to extend the commercial convention of 1815, and to make some agreement in regard to the slaves who had been carried off after the conclusion of the war, as well as with reference to the disputed northwestern boundary. His discussions with Lord Castlereagh, which are detailed at length in his diary, were fruitless, and the British Cabinet declined at that time to enter upon further negotiations. It may be inferred that although somewhat disturbed by the events of the war of 1812 they still did not think it worth while to take any steps toward improving their relations with the American people.

Soon after these conferences with Lord Castlereagh Mr. Adams returned to the United States in order to take his place in President Monroe's Cabinet on the 4th of March, 1817, and Mr. Rush succeeded him as Minister at London. Once more an effort to come to a further agreement on some, at least, of the outstanding questions was made, and Mr. Rush was instructed that if England would assent to a conference, Mr. Gallatin, who was our Minister at Paris, would be joined with him in the negotiations. Then it was that the effects of the war began to be really apparent. The exasperation caused by the seizure of our fishing vessels and by the refusal to carry out the provisions of the treaty of Ghent on the northwest coast made it evident that if something was not done the two countries would again be involved in hostilities. This danger, which would have made no impression upon the minds of British ministers ten years earlier, was now effective, and England's action showed that when it came to the point she was no longer ready to go to extremes. The Ministry changed its attitude and assented to a new negotiation. The result was the treaty of 1818, by which England admitted in principle the American contention that the fishing rights conceded in 1783 were final in their nature and could not be abrogated by war. Mr. Rush and Mr. Gallatin, moreover, succeeded in obtaining larger concessions in this respect than their instructions called for, and the American fishing rights within the three-mile limit, and also the right to dry and cure on the coast, were recognized as to certain portions of Newfoundland, Nova Scotia, and Canada. The treaty also disposed of the boundary from the Lake of the Woods to the Rocky Mountains, while from the

JOHN QUINCY ADAMS

(From the portrait by Copley)

mountains westward to the ocean the country was left open to the occupation of the subjects and citizens of both Powers for a term of ten years. The commercial convention was extended, and provision was made for the settlement of American claims on account of the slaves, who had been carried away, by referring the whole matter to the decision of some friendly sovereign. Nothing was said about the subject of seamen's rights, which had been so largely the cause of the war. The treaty of 1818 was as silent on this topic as the treaty of Ghent, but this question had in reality been settled by the war itself, for England, having found that the theme was one upon which the United States was always ready to fight, quietly allowed her claims in this direction to die away.

Four years after the treaty of 1818, and in accordance with the fifth article, the question of compensation for slaves or other property carried away after the war was referred to the Emperor of Russia, as arbitrator, and the Emperor's award decided that the United States was entitled to just indemnification for all such private property taken by the British forces, and more especially for all such slaves as were carried away from the places and territories for the restitution of which the treaty stipulated. The adoption of the treaty of 1818 was also the signal for the restoration to the United States of Astoria and the other points on the coast of the extreme Northwest. In this way the treaty of 1818, and the award of the Emperor of Russia, which grew out of it, brought the relations of the two countries into a better condition than they had enjoyed since the close of the American Revolution, and these treaties may be said to have constituted the first step toward the improvement of those relations which were destined to grow better, although with many checks and hindrances, for one hundred years to come.

The two countries were also drawn nearer together by holding the same attitude in regard to the revolting colonies of Spain in

South America, and by their common dislike and distrust of the principles of the Holy Alliance. When Canning broke away from the somewhat musty Toryism which thought everything was to go on just as of old, and as if the French Revolution had never happened, he not only powerfully aided the South American republics, but he greatly strengthened the position of the United States. Canning did not at all approve the extended form which his policy took on in the Monroe Doctrine, but his work could not be undone, and a common sympathy and a common policy in the South American struggle for freedom drew Great Britain and the United States closely together in the eyes of the world, and, also, although to a less degree, in their own estimation.

After the award of the Emperor in regard to indemnity for the slaves carried off by the British forces in the war of 1812, there was, with the exception of the conventions of 1827, renewing and extending the treaty of 1818 and providing for an arbitration of the disputed northeastern boundary, no international transaction involving serious differences, and no treaty between the two Governments of Great Britain and the United States, for twenty years. The marked effect which the war of 1812, as I have pointed out, had produced upon the attitude of England toward the United States was, however, very largely confined to the intercourse of the two Governments. That intercourse had become what, in diplomatic parlance, is termed "correct," and the old tone, so familiar in British despatches before the war of 1812, when the Ministry treated the United States as if it were a collection of African tribes and therefore not entitled to the ordinary good manners of international relations, wholly disappeared. Officially we had forced our way into the family of nations, and had secured the customary courtesies which international intercourse demands. Yet this improvement, which was of the first importance, did not go very far toward altering the feeling which existed among the peoples of the two countries toward each other. Our relations with Great Britain after the treaty of 1818 entered upon another phase quite outside the scope of governmental action, which in its result did more lasting harm to the cause of genuine friendship between the two nations than all the best efforts of diplomatists or public men on either side could remedy or undo.

Prior to the war of 1812 many books and much writing in reviews and newspapers appeared in England which treated of the United States in the most unfavorable manner, and in a spirit which at times might fairly be called malignant. This systematic defamation was carried on so generally and so persistently that it gave rise to a fixed belief in the United States not only that it was part of a deliberate plan, but that some of the writers, like Moore, Ashe, and Parkinson, were actually in the pay of the British Government, and that they wrote for the purpose of inflaming English hostility toward everything American, and of preventing emigration to England's former colonies. During those early years of the century the people of the United States seem to have had the good sense to treat these criticisms with indifference; and when the controversy between the countries culminated in war, printed attacks fell, in the presence of real fighting, unnoticed from the press. After the war, however, and after the settlement of the commercial relations of the two countries by the treaty of 1818, the habit of depreciating and libelling the United States, either in books or in more ephemeral publications, entered upon a new phase. Any one who will take the trouble to examine what was written in England about the United States during the period from 1820 to 1850 will find it difficult to avoid the belief that the assaults upon the American people were systematic in their nature. Those who are curious in such matters can find an excellent summary in Mr. McMaster's history, where the English comments upon the United States from 1820 to 1840 are vividly described. It seems almost incredible that such things could have been said and written by one ostensibly friendly people about another people who spoke the same language and inherited the same political traditions. There were, without doubt, many things in the United States of that day which were open to just and severe criticism. No successful defence, for example, could be entered before the tribunal of the civilized world in behalf of negro slavery. But the English critics did not confine themselves to that which was deserving of criticism. Everything in the United States was to them anathema. The great reviews gave many pages to depicting what the United States was as they beheld and interpreted it. Robert Southey in the "Quarterly," and Sydney Smith in the "Edinburgh," were only two of the most distinguished among the many writers great and small who devoted themselves not merely to criticising but to slandering the United States. They were not ashamed to effect their purpose by telling the most absolute falsehoods, and the lengths to which they went seem now well-nigh incredible. The men of America were said to be "turbulent citizens, abandoned Christians, inconstant husbands, unnatural fathers, and treacherous friends." The men who had whipped English vessels in eleven single ship fights out of thirteen were accused of having run away shamefully when they could not fight to advantage. As they generally fought to advantage at sea, they had not often run away. "In the Southern parts of the Union," says another calm thinker and judicious critic, "the rites of our holy faith are almost never practised; one-third of the people have no church at all. The religious principle is gaining ground in the northern parts of the Union. It is becoming fashionable among the better orders of society to go to church." It is interesting to consider this picture of church-going becoming fashionable among the descendants of the Puritans, but the writers had forgotten, probably, that New England

SYDNEY SMITH

CHARLES DICKENS

ROBERT SOUTHEY

was settled when it was a wilderness by people who went there, as Carlyle puts it, because they wanted to hear a sermon preached in their own way. "The supreme felicity of a true-born American is inaction of body and inanity of mind," is another description of the people of the United States, and the reproach of inactivity is one of the most comic ever addressed to Americans even at that time. Then, of course, the British critics had a great deal to say about our total lack of literature and the entire absence among us of any men of distinction. Franklin, we were informed, had elicited some useful discoveries, but that was because he had lived in England for some time. It might be suggested that there were many other persons dwelling in England whose residence in that favored island had failed to make them capable of eliciting Franklin's useful discoveries. It was also predicted that he would not be remembered for fifty years. Prophecies of fame are always perilous, and it is to be feared that Franklin is a good deal better remembered to-day than Sydney Smith or Southey — the most considerable of our critics in those days — and more read, too, if we may judge from the fact that every civilized nation not long since sent eminent representatives to Philadelphia to celebrate the two hundredth anniversary of his birth, a ceremony which seems to have been omitted in the case of Southey and Sydney Smith when a century had elapsed after their coming into the world. Robert Fulton, it was asserted, stole his invention from seeing the sailing ships which ran on the Clyde with steam-power in 1787, although no mention is made elsewhere of the persons who performed that feat, which does not seem to have travelled beyond the Clyde, and which is just as veracious as the statement, also made at that time, that Fulton was born in Paisley in Scotland, when in reality he had the misfortune to be born in Pennsylvania.

It is pleasant to think and it is only fair to

remember that at the very time when this railing against Americans was at its height, a man of genius, one of the great minds of England in those days, saw the injustice and folly of all this abuse and could speak of the American people not only temperately but kindly. Coleridge in his familiar talk refers to the United States and its people in this way:

"I deeply regret the anti-American articles of some of the leading reviews. The Americans regard what is said of them in England a thousand times more than they do anything said of them in any other country. The Americans are excessively pleased with any kind or favourable expressions, and never forgive or forget any slight or abuse. It would be better for them if they were a trifle thicker-skinned." . . .

"The last American war was to us only something to talk or read about; but to the Americans it was the cause of misery in their own homes." . . .

"I, for one, do not call the sod under my feet my country. But language, religion, laws, government, blood, — identity of these makes men of one country."[1]

And again on April 10, 1833, he said:

"The possible destiny of the United States of America, — as a nation of a hundred millions of freemen, — stretching from the Atlantic to the Pacific, living under the laws of Alfred, and speaking the language of Shakespeare and Milton, is an august conception. Why should we not wish to see it realized? America would then be England viewed through a solar microscope: Great Britain in a state of glorious magnification! How deeply to be lamented is the spirit of hostility and sneering which some of the popular books of travels have shown in treating of the Americans! They hate us, no doubt, just as brothers hate; but they respect the opinion of an Englishman concerning themselves ten times as much as that of a native of any other coun-

[1] Table Talk, May 28, 1830, "The Americans."

try on earth. A very little humouring of their prejudices, and some courtesy of language and demeanour on the part of Englishmen, would work wonders, even as it is, with the public mind of the Americans." ...

"Captain Basil Hall's book is certainly very entertaining and instructive but, in my judgment, his sentiments upon many points, and more especially his mode of expression, are unwise and uncharitable. After all, are not most of the things shown up with so much bitterness by him merely national foibles, parallels to which every people has and must of necessity have?"[1]

One feels disposed to say to-day that the slander and vilification by Sydney Smith and Southey, and by the pack of unknown writers who followed their example, is more than compensated by the kind, wise words of Coleridge, especially as Coleridge is still read and remembered, while the others, with the exception of Sydney Smith, are

[1] "Table Talk."

quite forgotten and their books and articles are to the world at large as unknown as if they had never existed. But at the time the words of those who defamed were printed and read, while Coleridge's talk was still unpublished.

These few passages which I have quoted from the Reviews give, however, a very faint impression of English criticism upon America at that time, although such stuff is hardly to be dignified by the name of criticism. It was in reality childish and rather ignorant abuse. But now, contrary to what had happened in the earlier years, the Americans, unfortunately, were roused into taking it up and making elaborate replies. They had not much difficulty in controverting the false statements and misrepresentations so freely made, but they did not stop there. They naturally availed themselves of the *tu quoque* argument, and it was not at all difficult in the history of England to find facts which, with appropriate twists and bendings, made the

English people appear in a very unenviable light.

This warfare of books and magazine articles continued and was much emphasized and embittered when it was waged on a large scale by popular writers like Mrs. Trollope and Captain Hall. Everything else, however, sank into insignificance compared to the effect of one book, much more temperate than any of the others, but written by a great genius who saw fit later to sharpen what he had said in a book of travels by carrying his animosity into the realms of fiction. Charles Dickens came to the United States in 1841. He was received with an outburst of affectionate and admiring enthusiasm which has rarely been seen anywhere in the case of a man of letters. He went home and wrote a book about us called " American Notes," and then he immortalized certain types of American character in "Martin Chuzzlewit." He said a great deal that was very true and entirely deserved. The characters of the novel were unfortunately in many respects only too real, and, deeply angered as we were at the time, it may be safely said that Elijah Pogram and Jefferson Brick and Hannibal Chollop, General Choke and Mrs. Hominy have an immortality more assured among the American people than anywhere else, for the anger has long since died away, while the truth of the satire and the comicality of those beings created by the magic touch of genius still remain. But at the time the resentment was intense. How intense the feeling was we can see from the following entry made by Emerson in his journal on November 25 (1842).

"Yesterday I read Dickens' 'American Notes.' It answers its end very well, which plainly was to make a readable book, nothing more. Truth is not his object for a single instant, but merely to make good points in a lively sequence, and he proceeds very well. As an account of America it is not to be considered for a moment: it is too short, and too narrow, too superficial, and too ignorant, too slight, and too fabulous, and the man totally unequal to the work. A very lively rattle on that nuisance, a sea voyage, is the first chapter; and a pretty fair example of the historical truth of the whole book. We can hear throughout every page the dialogue between the author and his publisher, — 'Mr. Dickens, the book must be entertaining — that is the essential point. Truth? Damn truth! I tell you, it must be entertaining.' As a picture of American manners nothing could be falser. No such conversations ever occur in this country in real life, as he relates. He has picked up and noted with eagerness each odd local phrase that he met with, and, when he had a story to relate, has joined them together, so that the result is the broadest caricature; and the scene might as truly have been laid in Wales or in England as in the States. Monstrous exaggeration is an easy secret of romance. But Americans who, like some of us Massachusetts people, are not fond of spitting, will go from Maine to New Orleans, and meet no more annoyances than we should in Britain or France. So with 'yes,' so with 'fixings,' so with soap and towels; and all the other trivialities which this trifler detected in travelling over half the world. The book makes but a poor apology for its author, who certainly appears in no dignified or enviable position."[1]

Emerson was not only a great man and a man of genius but he had one of the coolest, calmest, and best-balanced minds conceivable. Yet he could write in this fashion of the "American Notes." If Emerson felt in this way, and of course there is much truth in what he says, we can imagine the feelings of the average American about Dickens at that moment. Whether what was said in the "Notes" or in "Martin Chuzzlewit" at a later day was just or unjust, true or untrue, there was a widespread feeling in the United States that, whoever else might find fault with and ridicule us, Charles Dickens, after

---

[1] Emerson's Journals, 1841–1844, pp. 312–313.

the reception which had been given him, was debarred by every rule of loyalty and good manners from doing so. That this feeling was natural and that the rule was one which could be both accepted and observed was made visible to all men not long after the visit of Dickens.

A few years later another great English novelist came to the United States; came twice, in fact, and delivered lectures. No doubt, with his keen and penetrating observation, he perceived many things which lent themselves to criticism, to ridicule, and to satire, of which no living writer was more capable than he. He was by temperament very sensitive to just those shortcomings which are common and repellent in a crude and unformed society. He was urged in every way and tempted with the promise of great profits to write a book about America, but he declined. He had been cordially received in the United States; he had lived in our houses; he had accepted our hospitality; only kindness had been shown him.

Others might write what they pleased about America, but he would not. Let me recall what he himself said in a "Roundabout" paper:

"Yonder drawing was made in a country where there was such hospitality, friendship, kindness, shown to the humble designer that his eyes do not care to look for faults or his pen to note them. . . . How hospitable they were, those Southern men! In the North itself the welcome was not kinder, as I, who had eaten Northern and Southern salt, can testify!"

How kind and generous it all is, and how pleasant it is now, to every one who loves the memory of the genius that created Becky Sharp and drew the character of Colonel Newcome, to know that he was, above all things, loyal and true. We had on our own side, too, a distinguished man of letters whose conception of his duty toward the two nations who read his books was to cherish friendship and kindliness and not to seek for faults and embitter feelings. Let me describe him in Thackeray's words, for they both thought alike in this great matter which involves nothing less than good-will among men:

"Two men, famous, admired, beloved, have just left us, the Goldsmith and Gibbon of our time. . . . One was the first Ambassador whom the New World of Letters sent to the Old. He was born almost with the republic; the *pater patriæ* had laid his hand on the child's head. He bore Washington's name; he came amongst us bringing the kindest sympathy, the most artless, smiling good-will. His new country (which some people here might be disposed to regard rather superciliously) could send us, as he showed in his own person, a gentleman who, though himself born in no very high sphere, was most finished, polished, easy, witty, quiet; and, socially, the equal of the most refined Europeans. If Irving's welcome in England was a kind one, was it not also gratefully remembered? If he ate our salt, did he not pay us with a thankful heart?

Who can calculate the amount of friendliness and good feeling for our country which this writer's generous and untiring regard for us disseminated in his own? His books are read by millions of his countrymen; whom he has taught to love England, and why to love her. It would have been easy to speak otherwise than he did; to inflame national rancors, which, at the time when he first became known as a public writer, war had just renewed; to cry down the old civilization at the expense of the new; to point out our faults, arrogance, shortcomings, and give the republic to infer how much she was the parent state's superior. There are writers enough in the United States, honest and otherwise, to preach that kind of doctrine. But the good Irving, the peaceful, the friendly, had no place for bitterness in his heart, and no scheme but kindness."

Unfortunately, the example of Irving and Thackeray had but few imitators. Everything which these two said and wrote or omitted to say and write was forgotten in

WASHINGTON IRVING

WILLIAM MAKEPEACE THACKERAY

JAMES BRYCE

the clash of men who took a precisely opposite course, to the great detriment of all concerned, and the bitterness was concentrated around the "American Notes" and their author, whom the American people had loved and honored and taken to their hearts. It was this feeling that the man whom they had admired and cheered and feasted had been disloyal which made Dickens's criticism and ridicule rankle more than that of all others. But if we leave the personal equation aside, Dickens was only the culmination of the general commentary which England then made and apparently thought it well to make upon the United States. Both people spoke and read the same language. In those days they were still closely akin. We read English books, copied English fashions, and looked up to English standards in society and in literature, and therefore all that was said in England of the kind which has just been indicated went home and made Americans very angry and very sore. We were a new people, or rather we were the offspring of an old people settled in a new country, and we were young, very self-conscious, very sensitive, and we felt attacks which would be no more noticed to-day than the rattle of a dead autumn leaf fluttering before the wind. We replied to the criticisms in a savage and intemperate manner. Sometimes we wounded; generally we produced no effect. What we felt most was the injustice of painting everything black. As I have already said, there was a great deal in America to be criticised. Dickens's wrath about copyright, for instance, was wholly justifiable. Our own literary possessions were still meagre, and so we stood like highwaymen along the roadside of literature and robbed the passers-by, the very men who "helped us to enjoy life or taught us to endure it." To plunder others in this fashion was not only indefensible but most dishonest. The default on the State bonds, especially upon those of Pennsylvania, which edged the blade of Sydney Smith, who was a personal loser, was likewise indefensible, and was also utterly discreditable. To the great reproach of slavery there was, of course, no reply, no excuse to be made. But these dark spots were not the whole picture, and yet by gross misrepresentation, and even by actual falsehood, the effort was made to prove that everything was black. For instance, in " Martin Chuzzlewit " the impression is sedulously and strongly given that the entire United States west of the Alleghanies is one huge swamp breathing forth fever and ague. One has but to look at the illustrations of Mrs. Trollope's book to see the country Dickens described, and it would almost seem as if the American chapters in "Martin Chuzzlewit" were written "up" to Mrs. Trollope's pictures. No doubt such ugly and unwholesome spots existed then, and exist now, but as a description of so large a country as the United States it was not strictly accurate. Yet this was the prevailing tone. Everything was bad — land, people, institutions. The result naturally was that the just criticism had no effect and was merely lost in the cloud of invective and abuse. Many of the deficiencies were those which time alone could supply, but this was not stated any more than it was admitted that there was also in America much that was good and not a little that was great. In the days when we were still colonies Edmund Burke and the elder Pitt pictured the people of America and what they had achieved in language to which Parliament listened then, and which the world has heeded ever since. In the first half of the nineteenth century the American people were engaged in the conquest of a continent; they were bringing a wilderness within the grasp of civilized man, and at the same time they were making a great experiment in government, and had established religious freedom and individual liberty on a scale never known before. Their political example had affected the entire Western world, and this was really the underlying reason for the attacks upon them,

Reproduced from Mrs. Trollope's "Domestic Manners of the Americans."

WOOD CUTTER'S CABIN ON THE MISSISSIPPI

because their success alarmed the ruling classes of England and of Europe, which were likewise the vocal classes, in command of the press and the platform. None the less, these endeavors and achievements in that great new world were quite as worthy of note as our crude manners, our rough ways on the Western frontier, our lack of the luxuries of wealth, and of the many other lesser things in which we fell short of the European standards. But the good was never noticed and the bad was exaggerated beyond the bounds of truth. With the exception of what Dickens and Sydney Smith wrote, everything then said and written about the United States and its people is quite forgotten, except by the historian, and is as dead to the world as the nun who has taken the black veil. But looking back over that time, the period of the English commentators on America, one can see very plainly now the infinite mischief which was done. In point of taste and good feeling there is little to choose between the English attacks upon the United States and those of Americans upon England, although we had the great disadvantage of feeling much more keenly about it than our adversaries. Yet England herself was sensitive enough when Emerson and Hawthorne, two really great writers, ventured, in the most perfectly proper and temperate way, to point out that in certain respects the English people were, after all, merely human. Emerson and Hawthorne, of course, are still read and remembered, quite as much if not so widely as Dickens, but they do not come within the class that I have been trying to describe. They were later, and their tone was larger and more modern, their criticism more subtle, their praise ample, and their temper fair. During the time which I have attempted to portray the harm done was very great. Englishmen gave comparatively little attention to us or to what we thought or said, but the attacks of her writers upon the United States, running

Reproduced from Mrs. Trollope's "Domestic Manners of the Americans."

THE SOLEMNITY OF JUSTICE

through a period of years, bred a bitter hatred of England among the American people, which has gradually and fortunately grown into a cold but cheerful indifference, and this, in turn, it is to be hoped, will become something more and better than occasional friendship between individual members of the two nations.

The regret which one feels as one looks back over the writings of that period brimming over with bitterness and anger is enhanced by considering the good which might have been done by more serious works conceived in a different spirit. We have two conspicuous examples of such books ready to our hands and possessed of an enduring reputation denied to those who wrote of the United States only to decry and wound. De Tocqueville is of the same period. His famous book is by no means filled with undiluted praise. He both warned and criticised, but he took America seriously and he was studied and admired. In our own time a distinguished English statesman has written a book upon our body politic and our methods of government. He has seen what was good as well as what was evil in our politics and our political system. He is a severe but just judge. Far from resenting his strictures, Americans regard his book with admiration and as high authority. It may be truly said that no Englishman has ever been more popular in the United States than James Bryce, the author of the " American Commonwealth."

The final question which arises in one's mind when contemplating that time in the dry, cool light of history is whether, on the whole, it benefited England and was profitable to her to breed enmity and bitterness in a country which had every natural disposition to be her friend. The Government had ceased to aim deliberately at alienating the United States after the treaty of Ghent was made; and then it was that English writers, great and small, took up the work which the Government, for the time at least, had abandoned. Their operations were less dangerous because the issues of peace and war did not lie in their hands, but in creating a settled hate on the part of one people for another they were more effective than diplomatists and ministers, because they wounded personal pride and made each member of the community, according to his temperament, feel humiliation or anger, in his own particular person. To-day such writings on the part of the English or of any other nation would produce no effect of the slightest consequence in the United States. After nations pass a certain point in their rise to greatness abuse by inhabitants of other countries may make the person uttering the abuse unpopular, but has no effect upon the nation or people abused. Between 1820 and 1850, when the United States was still struggling in the first stages of nation-building, when it was still largely a wilderness and its pioneers were forcing the frontier westward with daring and painful effort, this abusive and savage criticism, whether just or not, was deeply felt.

That it had an improving or instructive effect upon Americans, in view of the manner in which the instruction was administered, may well be doubted, but in making them angry and in turning them against England, and causing them to look with the friendly eyes of preference on almost every other nation, it was highly successful. In the relations of two great nations, speaking the same language and believing in the same political principles, it is not a pleasant period to look upon in the clear light of seventy years later; yet I think, if rightly considered, it is not without its lesson, not only to those concerned, but to all who wish to maintain good relations among the nations of the earth.

During this same period, which may be called, as I have said, the period of the commentators and the critics, certain events occurred of a much more perilous nature, which brought the two countries to the verge of war. In the nature of things, we were certain to have many more matters of difference with Great Britain than with any other country, because her provinces lay to the north of the United States and furnished a common boundary line three thousand miles in length. What was much worse was the fact that this boundary line was left largely unsettled by the treaties of 1818 and 1827. One of the three treaties of 1827 provided for arbitration as to the northeast boundary, and the question was referred to the King of Holland as arbitrator. In 1831 the King rendered a decision, but as he really decided only two points and merely expressed an opinion as to all the others, his award was rejected by the United States upon the ground that it was not a decision of the questions submitted. Thus the entire matter was left open, and serious troubles soon began to arise along the northeastern boundary between the people of Maine on the one side and those of the adjoining British provinces on the other. An American surveyor was arrested. The State of Maine appropriated money and sent a force of men in Aroostook County to the border. There were similar difficulties in Madawaska. The English Government postponed action, and the question began to assume a very angry and threatening appearance. Meanwhile another disturbance broke out along the New York and Vermont frontiers. There had been a rebellion in Canada against the bad government of that day, and the defeated patriots took refuge in the United States, where they met with a cordial reception. Considerable bodies of volunteers were raised. Secret organizations were formed to support the rebellious Canadians, a party of whom, under the leadership of William McKenzie, seized Navy island, in the Niagara river, and fortified it. The authorities in Canada despatched Colonel McNab to guard the frontier against this invasion, and McNab sent out a party of armed men who seized and burned the steamer *Caroline*, which had been used to convey volunteers and munitions of war to Navy island. The destruction of the *Caro-*

line took place at Fort Schlosser, on American territory, and was, of course, a gross violation of the sovereignty of the United States. The Government of the United States and the State governments behaved, fortunately, with entire propriety and broke up and checked, so far as they could, the movements of the patriots and their sympathizers. Nevertheless, acts of violence continued on both sides. A party of refugees in the Thousand Islands crossed to the Canadian side and burned the steamer *Sir Robert Peel* as a set-off for the *Caroline*, while the American steamer *Telegraph* was fired upon. It would require a volume of reasonable size to give a history of these border troubles, which are not without much human interest, but which have all fallen quite dim now, and indeed are hardly remembered except by the historian. In a brief review of the relations of England and the United States during one hundred years it is impossible to do more than allude to them. It must suffice to say here that the whole border from Maine to Michigan was not only disturbed, but in a most inflamed and explosive condition. It was just one of those situations where war might have been precipitated at any moment by reckless men who were quarrelling over the possession of land and where a rebellion existed in one country which excited warm sympathy in the other. In addition, a case arose, growing out of the destruction of the *Caroline*, which aroused animosities even more than the actual troubles along the border. An American named Durfee had been shot and killed on the *Caroline*. Two years later a Canadian named Alexander McLeod came down from Canada and while he was drunk bragged of having himself killed Durfee. He was, of course, arrested, although it was afterwards shown that he had not been present at the destruction of the *Caroline*. But on his own admission it was perfectly proper to arrest him. The crime had been committed on American soil and McLeod had confessed himself to be the guilty man, yet none the less the English Government flew into a fine rage and undertook to interfere with the action of the courts. Not content with this, they also saw fit to offer their advice in regard to the case of the *Amistad*, a Spanish vessel which had been seized by the slaves whom she was carrying and had been run ashore at Long Island, where she was taken possession of by the Government. There was a very grave question as to what was to be done with the negroes, but no part of the question concerned England the least in the world, and her benevolent advice, coming just at that moment, was deeply resented. In this condition of public sentiment, with England on the edge of declaring war on account of McLeod, and with the popular feeling in the United States greatly excited by the border troubles and by the case of the *Amistad*, the Democrats went out of power and the Whigs came in, with Mr. Webster as Secretary of State. The situation was one of extreme and dangerous complexity. The British having avowed the destruction of the *Caroline* to be a Governmental act, it was obvious that McLeod could not properly be held, but his case was in the State courts of New York, over the proceedings of which the United States had no control. Mr. Webster endeavored to secure the discharge of McLeod, but in vain, and the New York courts refused to grant a writ of habeas corpus. On the other side, Mr. Fox, the British Minister, saw fit to adopt a most offensive tone, which Mr. Webster was the last man in the world to accept with tameness or in a meek spirit. He took a firm attitude with England, while suggesting privately that negotiations should be opened for establishing a conventional northeastern line, and, as has just been said, he used his best efforts to secure the discharge of McLeod. This perilous situation was fortunately relieved by two incidents which came to pass outside the efforts of the Government. McLeod was acquitted at Utica by the simple process of proving an alibi; and the Whigs

DANIEL WEBSTER

(From portrait in State Department)

were beaten in England, an event which made Lord Aberdeen Secretary of State for Foreign Affairs in place of Lord Palmerston. As has usually happened since the war of 1812, we fared much better with a Tory or Conservative administration than we did with Whigs or Liberals. Response was now made to Mr. Webster's proposal to establish a conventional line, and in January, 1842, information reached Mr. Webster from Mr. Everett that Lord Aberdeen had determined to assent to our proposition, and had sent Lord Ashburton as special Minister to the United States to settle the boundary and all outstanding questions. This marked a sharp change in the English attitude, and was no doubt owing in a measure at least to the confidence which was felt in Mr. Webster personally. Indeed, it is to Mr. Webster that we owe the settlement at this time of questions which had been so inflamed by extraneous and accidental circumstances as to have brought the two countries to the verge of war.

Mr. Webster's position had throughout been one of extreme difficulty. Not only did he have to deal with the McLeod case, but the border was in a constant ferment and he was compelled to be constantly on the alert to prevent, if possible, outbreaks which might precipitate hostilities at any moment. In addition to all this his own personal situation was most trying. General Harrison, who had made him Secretary of State, died a month after his inauguration, and, although President Tyler gave his entire confidence to Mr. Webster, he immediately broke with the Whig party, which had elected him, and Mr. Webster's position became, in consequence, a very difficult one. The Whigs felt that he ought immediately to resign. He was denounced as a traitor to Whig principles, and there was much bitterness of feeling. Mr. Webster, however, understood the situation between this country and Great Britain better than any one else. He knew how dangerous it was. He felt, and rightly, that if any one was able to bring it to a peaceful conclusion he could, and that whatever his party associates might say or think, it was his plain duty to remain in the Cabinet until the English question was settled. Unmoved, therefore, by the attacks made upon him, he remained at his post, and it was well for the country that he did so. Lord Ashburton arrived in the United States on the 4th of April, 1842, and the result of his negotiations with the Secretary of State was the agreement known in history as the Webster-Ashburton treaty, which was concluded on the 9th of August, 1842, and proclaimed in the following November. This result, however, was not easily reached, for the settlement was surrounded by difficulties, owing to the fact that the territory of the two States of Maine and Massachusetts was involved, and Mr. Webster, therefore, could not deal with this territory with a free hand. It was very fortunate that Mr. Webster was a New England man, and his personal influence as well as the tact he displayed were most effective in managing the arrangements with the two States. It is not possible to follow the negotiations in their details, for the discussion involved filled volumes at the time and might be made to fill volumes now. All that it is possible to say here is that the treaty brought about, in the first place, a condition of entire peace between the two countries and thus put an end to one in which war was momentarily probable. It settled the northeastern boundary and the northern boundary from Lake Huron to the Lake of the Woods, together with various matters related to these two questions. It also made an agreement for joint effort toward the suppression of the slave trade and for joint remonstrances to the other Powers against that traffic. It further provided in another article for the extradition of criminals. As a whole the treaty was a most important advance toward the establishment of good relations between the two branches of the English-speaking people. It was one of Mr. Webster's greatest achievements, and, in view of the extreme

LORD ASHBURTON

(From portrait in State Department)

irritation existing and the incipient border warfare, it was a very remarkable feat. Benton denounced the treaty in the Senate as a surrender to England, and Lord Palmerston assailed it in Parliament as a surrender by England to the United States; from which it may be inferred that it was, upon the whole, a very fair settlement.

The Webster-Ashburton Treaty had, however, one defect; it did not determine our northwestern boundary beyond the Rocky Mountains. That region, it will be remembered, under the treaties of 1818 and 1827 was left to the joint occupation of Great Britain and the United States, although Mr. Monroe had offered to end the dispute by adopting the forty-ninth parallel as the line of division. The country for some time remained unsettled, but the Hudson Bay Company finally started to push its posts down to the Columbia River, and just when Mr. Webster was at work on the treaty with Lord Ashburton the American movement toward Oregon began in earnest. As soon as our settlers arrived there troubles at once arose, and the question drifted into the domain of politics. The failure of the Webster-Ashburton Treaty to deal with it and the absorption of the Administration in the much greater question of the annexation of Texas kept the whole matter open with increasing irritation, although Mr. Tyler renewed the offer of the forty-ninth parallel, to which Great Britain paid no attention. The American rights and claims were taken up with noisy enthusiasm in different parts of the country, and were put forward by public meetings in the largest possible way. When the election of 1844 came on, the Democrats took extreme ground in their platform, claiming the whole region which was in dispute, and the cry of "Fifty-four forty or fight" ran through the campaign. The excitement was enhanced by the failure of Congress to act, for there were many Senators and Representatives from the older parts of the country who regarded Oregon as worthless, and who resisted all efforts to take action in regard to it. Mr. Polk, the Democratic candidate, was one of the extremists on the question and in favor of the 54-40 line. Nothing could have been less desirable than this attitude. It is never well to threaten, and it is particularly undesirable to threaten unless you mean just what you say. The people who were responsible for the cry of "Fifty-four forty or fight" did not really intend to fight for that line, and therefore the cry was mere bluster for political purposes. It had, however, the effect of inflaming the question, so that there was talk of war on both sides of the Atlantic. When Mr. Polk came in, he took very extreme ground in his inaugural, which had, as was to be expected, a very bad effect in England, and increased the difficulty of a settlement. After all his bluster, however, Polk, with the very lame excuse that he was involved by the acts of his predecessor, renewed the offer of the forty-ninth parallel, which Mr. Pakenham, the British Minister, who was apparently about as judicious as Polk, promptly, and, as it afterward appeared, without authority, declined. President Polk in his Message asked Congress for authority to terminate the convention of 1827. Resolutions were passed and the convention was terminated. The situation had now become so threatening that Mr. Webster made a strong speech at Boston in which he denounced the folly of going to war with England on such a question and urged its proper settlement. The speech made a deep impression not only in England and America, but in Europe. Pakenham, under instructions from the Ministry, then renewed on his side the offer of the forty-ninth parallel, and the valiant Polk accepted it with the approval of Congress. The treaty of 1846 followed, by which the line to the coast was settled. We obtained the Oregon country and granted to Great Britain the right of navigation on the Columbia River. The loss of the region between the forty-ninth parallel and the line of 54–40 was one of the most severe which ever befell the

United States. Whether it could have been obtained without a war is probably doubtful, but it never ought to have been said, officially or otherwise, that we would fight for 54–40 unless we were fully prepared to do so. If we had stood firm for the line of 54–40 without threats, it is quite possible that we might have succeeded in the end; but the hypotheses of history are of little practical value, and the fact remains that by the treaty of 1846 we lost a complete control of the Pacific coast.

It is impossible, nor is it necessary here, to enter into the controversies which arose from the annexation of Texas and in which England took no little interest, but the great movement of expansion which characterized that period brought on another difference with England which at one time was very serious and which resulted in a treaty that was for many years a stumbling-block in the way of all plans for building an Isthmian canal. From the time of Monroe, Clay, and John Quincy Adams the construction of an interoceanic canal had been one of the cherished desires of the United States. It passed through many phases, involved as it was in the tortuous and revolutionary conditions of Central America, but the question finally came to a head after the annexation of Texas. Great Britain had always, despite treaties to the contrary, maintained a hold on the Mosquito Coast and was in the habit of exercising a protectorate over a person, whom she humorously called the "Mosquito King," selected from the worthless savages who inhabited that region. She now took advantage of this interest in the Mosquito Coast to take possession of San Juan, which was at the mouth of the river where it was planned to begin the Nicaragua Canal. On the other hand, the United States engaged in the work of making arrangements with the Central American republics and with Granada to get possession of the canal routes. It is not necessary to follow the treaties made by Mr. Hise and later by Mr. Squier in which they exceeded their instructions and secured for us everything we desired. With England at the mouth of the San Juan and indulging herself in the seizure of Tigre Island, and with the United States possessed of treaties entered into by the people of the countries through which the canal must pass, all the conditions were ripe for a very pretty quarrel, which thereupon duly arose. There is no necessity of following it in all its intricacies, but the result was a treaty hastily made by Sir Henry Bulwer, the British Minister, and Mr. Clayton, Secretary of State, in order to forestall action upon the Squier treaty by the Senate.

The treaty thus made in 1850 provided that neither the United States nor Great Britain should ever obtain or maintain for themselves any exclusive control over the ship canal, or maintain any fortifications, or assume or exercise any dominion over Nicaragua, Costa Rica, the Mosquito Coast, or any part of Central America. The treaty further provided for the neutrality of the canal in case of war and for the protection of its construction, which both Powers promised to facilitate. It also arranged for guarantees of neutrality and for invitations to other Powers to coöperate. This agreement settled the outstanding differences between England and the United States, but it was pregnant with other difficulties hardly less serious. In its nature it was an abandonment of the Monroe Doctrine, because it provided for bringing in European Powers to deal with a purely American question, and also made it impossible for either the United States or Great Britain to build a canal without mutual coöperation. In process of time it became necessary to get rid of this treaty, which was a most unwise one. It undoubtedly removed a subject of great irritation at the moment, but it did so by agreements which carried with them the seeds of future troubles, always a perilous price to pay for temporary relief.

Nevertheless the immediate effect was soothing, and the next transaction between the two Governments was the treaty of 1854, which established reciprocity with Canada, and which, as was said at the time, was floated through by Lord Elgin upon seas of champagne. Although this treaty in its practical operation proved a disappointment to the United States, it was at least a distinctly friendly arrangement and indicates how much relations between the United States and Great Britain, despite many vicissitudes, had improved since the war of 1812. This was shown even more emphatically a few years later when the Prince of Wales, then a boy of eighteen, came to the United States in the year 1860. Although the fateful election of that year was in progress and the country was torn by the political conflict, the Prince was received with the utmost cordiality by every one in authority from the President down, and with real enthusiasm by the people. That he carried away pleasant memories of America was made evident throughout his life, and especially after he came to the throne, by his kindliness and friendship not only toward the United States, but toward all Americans. What was more important at the time, the warmth of his reception in the United States deeply gratified the Queen and Prince Albert, and was not without a marked influence a year later when the relations of the two countries and the fate of the American Union were trembling in the balance.

The Elgin treaty, and, still more, the visit of the Prince of Wales just on the eve of the Civil War, came at a time when the people of the United States were so deeply absorbed in the slavery question at home that they had little thought to give to their relations with any foreign country. The passions aroused by the slavery struggle were rising to a fierce intensity and the dark clouds of secession and civil war were already gathering upon the horizon. With the coming of that war all that had been gained in the past years toward the establishment of permanent and really friendly relations between the two countries, which had been severed by the American Revolution, was lost in a moment. During the years which had elapsed between 1850 and 1860 the most severe reproach uttered by English lips against the United States was the continued maintenance of negro slavery. The reproach was bitterly felt because no answer, no explanation, no defence, was possible. Now the United States was plunged in civil war waged by the North for the preservation of the Union, and all the world knew that the cause of the North carried with it freedom to the slaves. The people of the Northern States felt that under these circumstances and in that hour of trial the sympathy of England would go out to them at once without either question or hesitation. To their utter surprise, the feeling of England, as expressed in her magazines and newspapers and by the governing classes, was, with very rare exceptions, uniformly hostile. The vocal part of English society seemed to be wholly in sympathy with the South, and the North could not learn until later that the silent masses of England were on the side of the Union and freedom. The bitterness of hatred then awakened by the utterances of the English press and English public men can hardly be realized to-day. Early in the struggle its intensity was manifested when the *Trent* affair occurred. The act of Wilkes in stopping the *Trent* and taking from her the Southern commissioners was, from the standpoint of the United States, entirely indefensible, inasmuch as it was a flat contradiction of the American doctrine for which the country had fought in 1812. Yet in 1861 the people of the Northern States hailed the action of Wilkes with

Copyright, 1911, *by Review of Reviews Company. Taken from* "*Photographic History of Civil War.*"

REAR ADMIRAL CHARLES WILKES, U.S.N.

wild delight, and the hatred aroused by the English attitude was so great that they were quite ready to go to war, although war at that moment probably meant the establishment of the Confederacy and the final severance of the Union.

It is not easy now to realize the intensity of the feeling or the fierce joy which broke out everywhere in the North when the stopping of the *Trent* with the Commissioners of the Confederacy was known. Mr. Charles Francis Adams, in his very thorough and most interesting paper upon the "Trent Affair," gives a vivid picture of the excitement and of the manifestations of public approval in Boston, whither Mason and Slidell had been brought for incarceration in Fort Warren. The Governor and the Chief Justice, Edward Everett, with his long career of public and diplomatic service, eminent lawyers, men of the largest business and financial interests vied with each other in applauding the taking of the commissioners from the *Trent*, and in sustaining the legality of the act. By Governor Andrew Mason and Slidell were compared unfavorably with Benedict Arnold, and Mr. Robert C. Winthrop was denounced as little better than a traitor because he sent some wine to the prisoners, whom he had known well in Washington, and who, shut up in a harbor fort in the midst of a New England winter, were certainly not enjoying an undue amount of comfort. Two days after his arrival a great banquet was given to Captain Wilkes, and his officers and the speakers, among whom were Governor Andrew and the Chief Justice, praised Wilkes in unmeasured terms and gloried in what had been done. Boston did not differ from the rest of the country, and if such was the feeling among the best-informed and most conservative classes of the community, it is not difficult to imagine what a wave of passionate exultation swept over the masses of the people throughout the North. The reason for all this emotion, and for the violent manifestations of it in speech and in the press, lay in the wild hatred of England, which had been aroused by the apparent attitude of her people, and by the language of her newspapers in our hour of trial, and was not at all due to the fact that two notorious Southern leaders had been captured. The fact that the *Trent* was an English ship was the cause of the reckless language and unbridled exultation of the American people in the loyal North who, regardless of consequences, rejoiced in this sharp retort to the insults which England was heaping upon the United States.

On the other hand, the English attitude in regard to the *Trent* affair was not calculated to improve this situation, although, in all candor, it must be said that it is difficult to see how England could have, practically, assumed any other position than that which she actually took, despite the fact that by so doing she utterly rejected the doctrine which she had upheld and enforced even at the cost of war during the first fifteen years of the century. The reversal of England's position and her rupture with the past were, at once, violent and complete. On November 11, 1861, Lord Palmerston wrote to Mr. Delane:[1]

"It may be useful to you to know that the Chancellor (Lord Westbury), Dr. Lushington, the three Law officers, Sir G. Grey, the Duke of Somerset, and myself, met at the Treasury to-day to consider what we could properly do about the American cruiser come, no doubt, to search the West Indian packet supposed to be bringing hither the two Southern envoys; and, much to my regret, it appeared that, according to the principles of international law laid down in our courts by Lord Stowell, and practised and enforced by us, a belligerent has a right to stop and search any neutral not being a ship of war, and being found on the high seas and being suspected of carrying enemy's

---

[1] Proc. Mass. Hist. Society, November, 1911, "The Trent Affair," by Mr. Charles Francis Adams, p. 54.

despatches; and that consequently this American cruiser might, by our own principles of international law, stop the West Indian packet, search her, and if the Southern men and their despatches and credentials were found on board, either take them out, or seize the packet and carry her back to New York for trial."

The opinion of November 11 so historically correct did not long endure. It was not difficult for the three Law officers of the Crown when the event actually occurred to slip away by a pleasing gyration from their opinion sustaining Lord Stowell and discover that the seizure of the *Trent* was indefensible because Wilkes had not taken the ship and sent her into a prize court. With this wholly preposterous proposition they managed to bridge over the gulf which separated the legal doctrine they had always cherished from that of the United States and the rest of the civilized world. These ingenious if flexible Law officers of the Crown were also able in this way to give the ministers the legal shelter necessary to protect them when they proceeded to act not in obedience to their doctrine steadily upheld for sixty years but in accord with their own desires and prejudices as well as with the sentiment and the passions of the English people at that moment. Feeling in England was as violent as in the United States and was quite as intemperately expressed. A single example, which is a statement in regard to Captain Wilkes, will show sufficiently the mental attitude of England and the degree of calmness which she exhibited. Captain Wilkes, it must be remembered, was a gentleman as well as an officer of distinction and reputation widely known by his antarctic expedition. The worst that could fairly be charged against him was that in the *Trent* affair he had acted hastily and without orders but in strict accord with the English doctrine as to the rights of neutrals and in direct contravention of the American doctrine on the same point in behalf of which the United States had gone

LORD PALMERSTON

to war half a century before. This conduct was injudicious, no doubt, but it was neither criminal nor disgraceful. Here is what the *London Times* said about Captain Wilkes and the American people in November, 1861:

" He is unfortunately but too faithful a type of the people in whose foul mission he is engaged. He is an ideal Yankee. Swagger and ferocity, built up on a foundation of vulgarity and cowardice — these are his characteristics, and these are the most prominent marks by which his countrymen, generally speaking, are known all over the world. To bully the weak, to triumph over the helpless, to trample on every law of country and custom, wilfully to violate all the most sacred interests of human nature, to defy as long as danger does not appear, and, as soon as real peril shows itself, to sneak aside and run away — these are the virtues of the race which presumes to announce itself as the leader of civilization and the prophet of human progress in these latter days. By Captain Wilkes let the Yankee breed be judged."

One knows not which to admire most, the moderation of this statement or the dignity with which it is expressed. It makes one think of the Eatanswill newspapers and of Pott and Slumkey, their immortal editors. Yet the *Times* was at that time not only the greatest and most powerful newspaper in England but the greatest and most powerful newspaper in the world. If the great mastiff of the English press could howl in this way, it is easy to imagine what the barkings and yelpings of Blanche, Tray and Sweetheart, and the rest of the little dogs must have been like.

With the popular mind both in England and the United States in this condition the situation was not only one of the utmost difficulty for the administration but was in a high degree perilous. The danger was enhanced by the fact that the popular feeling was rife among public men in Washington who were charged with the responsibility of office. Mr. Welles, the Secretary of the Navy, who if we may trust his diary never gave way to a generous emotion or praised any one if he could possibly help it, seized this occasion to send a despatch to Captain Wilkes approving and applauding what he had done in a most injudicious and extreme manner. Congress voted Wilkes a gold medal. Senator Sumner and Montgomery Blair the Postmaster-General indeed seem to have been the only men in Washington with one exception who from the beginning took a sane and thoroughly wise view of the capture of the Confederate envoys. That exception happily was the President himself, and his attitude was more vital just then than that of all other men in office put together. There was no doubt of his position or of his perfect clearness of vision from the very beginning. Mr. Lossing the historian saw the President just after the arrival of the despatch from Captain Wilkes announcing the capture of Mason and Slidell, and this is his account of the interview:

"The author was in Washington city when the news reached there of the capture of the conspirators, and he was in the office of the Secretary of War when the electrograph containing it was brought in and read. He can never forget the scene that ensued. Led by the Secretary, who was followed by Governor Andrew of Massachusetts, and others, cheer after cheer was given by the company with a will. Later in the day, the writer, accompanied by the late Elisha Whittlesey, First Comptroller of the Treasury, was favored with a brief interview with the President, when the clear judgment of that far-seeing and sagacious statesman uttered through his lips the words which formed the key-note to the judicious action of the Secretary of State afterward. 'I fear the traitors will prove to be white elephants,' said Mr. Lincoln. 'We must stick to American principles concerning the rights of neutrals. We fought Great Britain for insisting, by theory and practice, on the right to do precisely what Captain Wilkes

ABRAHAM LINCOLN

(From a photograph)

ONE HUNDRED YEARS OF PEACE

has done. If Great Britain shall now protest against the act, and demand their release, we must give them up, apologize for the act as a violation of our doctrines, and thus forever bind her over to keep the peace in relation to neutrals, and so acknowledge that she has been wrong for sixty years.'"[1]

Thus at once, even in the first moment of excitement, Mr. Lincoln grasped the situation and pointed out the true policy. Fifty years later it is easy to say what a chance was lost for an exhibition of the highest statesmanship in not at once making public dec-

---

[1] "The Civil War in America." Benson J. Lossing. Vol. II, pp. 156–157. Mr. Welles, Secretary of the Navy, corroborated the statement in *The Galaxy* for May, 1873, p. 647*: " The President, with whom I had an interview, immediately on receiving information that the emissaries were captured and on board the *San Jacinto*, before consultation with any other member of the cabinet discussed with me some of the difficult points presented. His chief anxiety — for his attention had never been turned to admiralty law and naval captures — was as to the disposition of the prisoners, who, to use his own expression, would be elephants on our hands that we could not easily dispose of. Public indignation was so overwhelmingly against the chief conspirators that he feared it would be difficult to prevent severe and exemplary punishment, which he always deprecated."

* "Abraham Lincoln, a History." Nicolay and Hay. Vol. V, p. 26.

laration of the position which Mr. Lincoln stated informally in his conversation with Mr. Lossing. Had he done so, he would probably have committed a blunder of the first magnitude. It was not difficult for other and lesser men to announce rash judgments or vow undying hatred of England on the one hand or on the other to express sound and wise opinions like Mr. Sumner and Mr. Blair. But upon the President, and upon the President alone, rested the dread responsibility of decision and action. He understood and gauged the feelings of the American people far better than any one else. He knew what a tempest of passionate excitement was sweeping over the country. It was so strong that Mr. Russell, the correspondent of the *London Times,* did not think that the government would dare to give up the prisoners and expected riot and disturbance if it was attempted. To have defied public feeling in its first wild outburst by announcing that Wilkes had done wrong and that the prisoners would be immediately given up would not have been statesmanship but a mad temptation of fate. The administration had only been in power a little more than six months. It was hedged in by perils, it was not strong, it had encountered a great disaster at the first battle of Bull Run; it was in no condition to stand the shock of popular wrath which would have been poured out upon it if it had undertaken to give up Mason and Slidell at once when the excitement and exultation of the public were at their height. Mr. Lincoln, therefore, sought for delay and suggested compromises. He secured the delay, forty days passed, the sober second thought asserted itself, Mr. Seward sent his memorable despatch, and Mason and Slidell were surrendered quietly and without outbreak of any kind. A month earlier this would have been impossible. On the other side of the Atlantic the situation was saved by the calm wisdom of the Prince Consort. The English Ministers were only too ready to take advantage of the *Trent* affair in order to precipitate a war which would have insured the destruction of the United States. Fortunately, however, they were persuaded by the wise counsels of Prince Albert, acting through the Queen, by whom American kindness to the Prince of Wales was still freshly remembered, to modify a despatch which, if unaltered, would almost certainly have brought on war and the establishment of the Confederacy. In his "History of Twenty-five Years" Sir Spencer Walpole says:

[1] ". . . Fortunately, while the passions of the multitude were excited, the judgment of two men of high station remained cool; for, on one side of the Atlantic, Mr. Lincoln had, from the first, the wisdom to see that Captain Wilkes's action could not be justified;[2] and, on the other side, the Prince Consort had the discretion to recommend

---

[1] "History of Twenty-five Years," by Spencer Walpole. Vol. II, p. 45.

[2] "Hansard," Vol. CLXV, p. 522. Cf., on the whole story, Lord Selborne, "Family and Personal Memorials," Vol. II, pp. 389 seq.

that the despatch which the Government had drawn up should be modified by the expression of a hope and a belief that Captain Wilkes's act was neither directed nor approved by the Government of the United States."[1]

Knowing from the moment when the news came what ought to be done and what must be done, Lincoln, with his large and patient wisdom, bided his time. The public excitement subsided, and then the President surrendered Mason and Slidell. The country, unconvinced, accepted his decision, but the real feeling of the people was exactly expressed in Lowell's lines :

"We give the critters back, John,
  Cos Abram thought 'twas right ;
It warn't your bullying clack, John,
  Provokin' us to fight.
Ole Uncle S. sez he, ' I guess
  We've a hard row,' sez he,
    ' To hoe jest now ; but thet somehow
  May happen to J. B.
  Ez wal ez you an' me.' "

---

[1] "Life of Prince Consort," Vol. V, p. 422. It ought to be added that Lord Lyons, on his own responsibility, extended by twelve hours the time alloted to the Government of the United States to give their reply. Sir E. Malet, "Shifting Scenes," p. 29.

The avoidance, by Lincoln's action, of this great peril did not, however, alter — on the contrary, it intensified — the hostile feeling of the loyal people of the North toward England, nor was there anything in the utterances or conduct of those who spoke for England calculated to produce a change. The vilification in the magazines and newspapers of the United States and her President and of all her leaders and soldiers continued without ceasing and without modification. From British ports and British shipyards armed vessels slipped away, which, although nominally ships of the Confederate navy, pursued in reality a simple career of privateering closely akin to piracy. The only one of them which actually came into action was destroyed by the *Kearsarge*, and an English yacht rescued the Southern officers and the British crew of the sinking *Alabama*. This business of furnishing a Confederate navy from the ports and shipyards of a neutral country was continued with the covert support of the British

Cabinet until the case of the Laird rams was reached.

The struggle which Mr. Adams carried on for many weary months not only against the British ministry but against the Law officers of the Crown, the bench, the bar, the vested interests, and the aristocracy of England is one of the most dramatic chapters in the whole history of the Civil War. The letters of Mr. Adams are a monument of ability, tenacity, courage, and force. The culmination came in September, 1863, when the rams were about to sail. On September 1st Lord Russell wrote that her majesty's government could not interfere with the sailing of the Rams. On September 3d, nothing of any importance having occurred since the letter of September 1st was despatched, Lord Russell ordered the Rams detained and notified Lord Palmerston, who was in Scotland, of his action. On the same day Mr. Adams wrote a note to Lord Russell containing a veiled ultimatum, so thinly veiled, indeed, that war appeared very plainly behind the diaphanous curtains of diplomatic words. On September 4 Lord Russell wrote Mr. Adams that the matter of the rams was under the most " serious and anxious consideration of her Majesty's government." Still ignorant that his victory was won, Mr. Adams sat down and wrote his famous note of September 5. To tell the story fittingly I will give it in the words of Mr. Brooks Adams, taken from his article upon the " Seizure of the Laird Rams," which is as admirable in form as it is thorough and complete in treatment.

"That day, September 3d, 1863, when Earl Russell's note declining to stop the rams, and Mr. Adams's note conveying a veiled ultimatum touching their sailing, crossed each other, marked a crisis in the social development of England and America. To Mr. Adams the vacillation of the Cabinet seemed astounding weakness. On September 8th he wrote to Seward: 'The most extraordinary circumstance attending this history is the timidity and vacillation in the assumption

LORD JOHN RUSSELL

(From a photograph)

of a necessary responsibility by the officers of the Crown.' To us, who look back upon the Civil War through a vista of fifty years, 'the most extraordinary circumstance' seems to be that terrible energy which enabled the United States in the extremity of her agony to coerce the nobility and gentry, the army, the navy, the church, the bench, the bar, the bankers, the ship-builders, the press, in fine, all that was wealthy, haughty, influential, and supposed to be intelligent in Great Britain. And it was as the vent of this energy that Mr. Adams, after receiving Earl Russell's letter of September 4th, wrote on September 5th, although despairing of success, his memorable declaration of war. Enclosing a paragraph cut from a Southern newspaper which contained the familiar threat of burning Northern ports with English-built ships, he observed as calmly as though he were summing up a mathematical demonstration:

"'It would be superfluous in me to point out to your Lordship that this is war. . . . In my belief it is impossible that any nation, retaining a proper degree of self-respect, could tamely submit to a continuance of relations so utterly deficient in reciprocity. I have no idea that Great Britain would do so for a moment.'"

It was a very great victory, as important to the United States and as decisive of the result as a hard fought battle, although it was won without bloodshed. The escape of the rams would certainly have seriously protracted the war and caused enormous losses to the United States. To have stopped them, as Mr. Adams did, was a remarkable feat and a signal service, but the action of England, extorted at the last moment, did not soften American hostility, even though English shipyards then ceased finally to send forth privateers.

In the great life and death struggle in which the people of the United States were engaged the loss of some merchant ships on the high seas was an injury so comparatively trifling in its effect upon the

CHARLES FRANCIS ADAMS

result that it was hardly perceptible; but the course of England which permitted the destruction of merchant vessels in this way, and which threatened by means of the Laird rams to break up the blockade, was, in the eyes of the American people, a crime of the first magnitude. The leaders of the English Cabinet were not friendly, although Lord Palmerston, fortunately for us, was more indifferent and less actively hostile than was generally supposed, and neither he nor Lord John Russell, who was much less friendly, was disposed to precipitate war. The one outspoken champion of the Confederacy was Gladstone; but fate so willed it that in striving to harm the United States he rendered it a great and decisive service. It was in the autumn of 1862, a very dark hour in the fortunes of the United States. The Ministry were preparing to recognize the Confederacy. The Queen, since the death of Prince Albert, as Mr. Charles Francis Adams has recently shown, had ceased to interest herself in American affairs.

A Cabinet meeting was called for October 23d, and then the recognition of the Confederacy was to be given. On the 7th of October Mr. Gladstone, anticipating the action of the Cabinet, went to Newcastle and delivered the famous speech in which he declared that "Jefferson Davis had made a nation." Lord Palmerston saw his successor in Gladstone, but he had no intention of letting him rule before his time. He resented the Newcastle speech; he did not propose to have Mr. Gladstone force his hand, and a week later he sent Sir George Lewis down to Hereford to controvert and disavow the Newcastle utterances. The Cabinet meeting on the 23d was postponed, but the accepted time had passed, and never returned. Mr. Gladstone's speech, however, did its work in the United States, still further embittering the already intense and deep-seated enmity toward England and her Government. We had friends, it is true — some even in the Cabinet, like Sir George Lewis — but the general attitude of the English Ministry was such that, while it inflamed the enmity of the North, it was far from gaining the friendship of the South, because, while the South was amused with sympathetic expressions and encouraged to hope for substantial support, it never received anything of real value, thus being left with an unpleasant sense of having been betrayed. A system more nicely calculated to incur the hostility of both sides in the great quarrel could not have been imagined, and it does not seem unjust to suggest that such a system did not imply a very high order of intelligence. Only very slowly and entirely outside the Government did it become apparent that the Union and freedom had any friends in England. The first public man to declare for the North was Richard Cobden, and he was followed by John Bright, whose powerful and most eloquent speech on the Roebuck resolution was one of the greatest services rendered by any man, not an American, to the cause of the Union. Lord Houghton, then Monckton Milnes, also spoke for us in the House of Commons. Mr. Forster was our friend, so were John Stuart Mill, Goldwin Smith, and Thomas Hughes; and there were others, of course, like these men, whose support it was an honor to have.

The working-men of Lancashire, reduced to misery by the cotton famine, were none the less true in their sympathy for the cause which they believed to be that of human rights and human freedom. But these voices, potent as they were, were lost in the general clamor which arose from the clubs of London, from the newspapers, and from the reviews. The desire to side actively with the South declined, of course, as the fortunes of the Confederacy sank, but the contemptuous abuse of the North went on without abatement. Even so late as the last year of the war as clever a man as Charles Lever demonstrated, in *Blackwood's Magazine,* to his own satisfaction the folly and absurdity of Sherman's great movement. The article appeared just in time to greet Sherman as he emerged triumphant at Savannah.

Sherman's march to the sea, following jeers and predictions like those put forth by Lever, produced a profound impression in England, which then, at last, seemed to become dimly conscious that a great war had been fought out by great armies. The end of the war and the complete triumph of the Union cause soon followed. As in games, so in more serious things, Englishmen are excellent winners, but, as a rule, poor losers, apt to cry out, when they have lost, that there has been something unfair, and to try to belittle and explain away their adversary's victory. In this case, however, England showed herself a good loser, for the result was too momentous to be treated with contempt or with charges of unfairness. Moreover, England found herself confronted not only by the success of the United States, and the consequent consolidation of the Union, but by a very unfortunate situation which she had herself created. She had managed to secure the bitter hostility of both sides. She had given sympathy to the South, but had done nothing practical for the cause of the Confederacy, and at the same time she had outraged the feelings of the Northern people and developed among them a bitterness and dislike which, when they were flushed with victory, might easily have had most serious consequences. It is quite true that she had not behaved so badly toward the United States as France, which had stopped just short of war. When England, France, and Spain united to exact reparation from Mexico, England and Spain withdrew as soon as they discovered that France intended to establish a government of her own creation upon Mexican soil. Not only was the French Government sympathetic with the South, but Napoleon was more than anxious to recognize the Confederacy, and took advantage of our civil war to fit out the Mexican expedition and establish Maximilian as Emperor. As soon as the war was over we forced France out of Mexico, and the unfortunate Maximilian, an amiable and brave man, of less than mediocre capacity, was executed by his subjects and thus offered up as a sacrifice to his incautious reliance upon the French Emperor and to his own ignorance of the peril of infringing the Monroe Doctrine.

Yet, despite all this, the people of the United States cared very little about what France had done, and felt bitterly all that the English had said. The attitude of the French Government during our Civil War, which there is no reason to suppose was the attitude of the French people, no doubt caused Americans generally to sympathize with Germany in the war of 1870, but except for that sympathy we regarded with great indifference the French treatment of the United States during the civil war. Very different was the case with Great Britain. As soon as the war was over the era of apology began on the part of England, finding its first expression in Tom Taylor's well-known verses upon the death of Lincoln. The acknowledgment of mistakes, however, produced but slight impression in the United States, where there was a universal determination to exact due reparation for the conduct of England, and especially for the depredations of the *Alabama* and the other cruisers let loose from British shipyards to prey upon our commerce. Attempts were at once made to settle these differences, but the Johnson-Clarendon treaty was rejected by the Senate, and when Grant came to the Presidency there was a strong feeling, represented by Mr. Sumner, in favor of making no demands upon England, but of obtaining our redress by taking possession of Canada. With a veteran army of a million men and a navy of over seven hundred vessels, including some seventy ironclads, the task would not have been a difficult one. President Grant and Mr. Fish, however, decided upon another course, and were genuinely unwilling to adopt a policy which, however justifiable, might have carried the country into another war. The result was that England sent out a special commission to Washington to make a treaty. Mr. Gladstone, who was then prime minister, behaved with manliness and courage. He admitted frankly the great mistake he had made in his Newcastle speech, and bent all his energies to reaching a settlement with the United States which would satisfy Americans and so far as possible heal the wounds inflicted by England's attitude and by English utterances during the war. In the first article of the treaty of 1871, which followed, it is said:

"Her Britannic Majesty has authorized her high commissioners and plenipotentiaries to express in a friendly spirit the regret felt by her Majesty's Government for the escape under any circumstances of the *Alabama* and other vessels from British ports and for the depredations committed by those vessels."

It must have been a serious trial, not only for a Ministry but for a proud and powerful nation, thus formally and officially to apologize for its past conduct, and yet, unless England was ready for war and for the loss of Canada, no other method seemed possible. It is greatly to England's credit and to the credit of Mr. Gladstone's Government that they were willing to express their regret for having done wrong.

The treaty established a court of arbitration to consider and pass upon the claims. It also provided for referring the differences in regard to the line of our boundary through the Fuca Straits to the Emperor of Germany, who subsequently made an award wholly in favor of the United States. The treaty also dealt with many other questions, including fishery rights, the navigation of the St. Lawrence and of Lake Michigan, the use of canals, and the conveyance of merchandise in bond through the United States. In due course the *Alabama* claims were taken before the Geneva tribu-

THE LAND OF LIBERTY

nal. The arbitration came dangerously near shipwreck, owing to the projection into it of the indirect claims, so called, which were urged in a powerful speech by Mr. Sumner in the Senate, but the tribunal wisely excluded them, and the case came to a decision, an award of $15,500,000 being made to the United States for the damages caused by the *Alabama* and her sister ships.

So far as the official relations of the two countries were concerned, the treaty of Washington restored them to the situation which had existed before the Civil War. Once again we were, officially speaking, on good and friendly terms with Great Britain, but the feeling left among the people of the United States by England's attitude remained unchanged, and the harsh and bitter things which had been said in England during our days of trial and suffering still rankled deeply. This was something which only the passage of time could modify, and the wounds which had been made took long to heal, although the healing process was facilitated by the fact that the civil war had made the people of the United States profoundly indifferent to foreign criticism. There was, moreover, no clash between the countries until many years after the treaty of Washington, and when the next difficulty arose it came not from any immediate difference between England and the United States, but grew out of an English invasion of the Monroe Doctrine in South America.

For many years there had been a dispute between England and Venezuela as to the boundary between that country and the possessions of England in British Guiana. Venezuela, weak and distracted by revolution, had sought more than once for arbitration, which England would not grant. On the contrary, the British Government had steadily pushed its line forward and extended its claims until it was found that it was gradually absorbing a large part of what had always been considered Venezuelan territory. Venezuela had broken off diplomatic relations, but nothing had succeeded in checking the English advances. The offer of the good offices of the United States had been equally fruitless, and when the matter finally reached a crisis, Mr. Cleveland, on December 17, 1895, sent in his well-known message. After reviewing the Venezuelan question and the efforts that we had made toward a peaceful settlement, the President recommended that an American commission be appointed to examine the question and report upon the matter. He said that when such report was made "it would be the duty of the United States to resist by every means in its power as a wilful aggression upon its rights and interests the appropriation by Great Britain of any lands or the exercise of governmental jurisdiction over any territory which after investigation we have determined of right belongs to Venezuela." The Message concluded with the following sentence: "I am, nevertheless, firm in my conviction that, while it is a grievous thing to contemplate the two great English-speaking peoples of the world as being otherwise than friendly competitors in the onward march of civilization and strenuous and worthy rivals in all the arts of peace, there is no calamity which a great nation can invite which equals that which follows a supine submission to wrong and injustice and the consequent loss of national self-respect and honor, beneath which are shielded and defended a people's safety and greatness." The language employed by the President was vigorous and determined. At the time it was thought rough. England was surprised, and operators in the stock market were greatly annoyed. The closing words of the message, which was a very able one, do not seem quite so harsh to-day as they did at the time when they were read to Congress. President Cleveland, moreover, however much Wall Street might cry out, had the country with him, and no one to-day, I think, can question the absolute soundness of his position.

With the existing possessions of any European Power in the Western Hemisphere we, of course, do not meddle, but it is the settled policy of the United States that those possessions shall not be extended or new ones created. The forcible seizure of American territory by a European Power would be, of course, an obvious violation of the Monroe Doctrine, which this country believes essential to its safety; but the gradual grasping of American territory on the basis of shadowy, undetermined, and constantly widening claims, differs from forcible seizure only in degree. If, in this case, the land in dispute belonged to Great Britain, we had nothing whatever to say, but so long as it was in controversy the United States had the right to demand that that controversy should be settled by a proper tribunal under whose decision the world should know just what belonged to England and what to Venezuela. President Cleveland's strong declaration surprised England, but it brought her to terms.

She woke up to the fact that the day had long since passed when the United States could be trifled with on any American question, and the soundness of Mr. Cleveland's judgment was shown by the fact that within a year the question was referred to a tribunal which met in Paris and which consisted of two Americans, two Englishmen, and one Russian jurist. The American judges were Chief Justice Fuller and Mr. Justice Brewer, of the Supreme Court. They went to Paris with the somewhat innocent idea that they were to hear the case and decide it on its merits, exactly as they decided a case in their own Supreme Court. They found, however, that the two English judges had no such conception of their functions, but were there as representatives of England, holding the positions of advocates instead of judges. The result was that the decision rested with the fifth man, Mr. Martens, and he, apparently under instructions not strictly judicial, was prepared to decide entirely in favor of England, although the English case for a large part of the claim was of the most shadowy character. It was very important, however, to England that the award should be signed by all the arbitrators, and that which was most essential to Venezuela was to preserve her control of the mouths of the Orinoco. The American arbitrators consented to sign the award if the mouths of the Orinoco were left to Venezuela, and this was done, all the rest of the disputed territory going to England. If the rest of the territory belonged to England, the mouths of the Orinoco also should have been hers. If the mouths of the Orinoco belonged to Venezuela, England was not entitled to a large part of what she received. In other words, the judgment of the arbitral tribunal was a compromise and not a decision on the merits of the case, in which it followed the course of most arbitrations and disclosed the weakness of which arbitral tribunals have hitherto nearly always been guilty. This failing is that they do not decide a case on its merits, but make a diplomatic compromise, giving something to each side. It is this tendency or practice of arbitral tribunals which has caused them to be distrusted, and especially in the United States, because, while the United States has no questions in Europe, Europe has many questions of interest in the Western Hemisphere, and the result has been on more occasions than one that the United States has been drawn into an arbitration where it could gain nothing and was certain to lose if any compromise was effected. In this particular instance, however, the result which Mr. Cleveland desired and which he sought to reach by his Message was fully attained. The boundary was determined, the process of gradual encroachment upon a weak American state under cover of claims more or less artificial and advanced by a powerful European nation was stopped, and an end was put once and for all to the plan of securing new American possessions by the insidious method of starting and developing claims and then refusing to have the claims settled and boundaries determined by any impartial tribunal. Mr. Cleveland rendered a very great public service by his action and caused the Powers of Europe to understand and appreciate the force and meaning of the Monroe Doctrine as they had never done before.

Three years after President Cleveland's Venezuelan Message the United States was at war with Spain. Admiral Dewey's fleet had captured Manila and the great European Powers hastened to send war-ships to the scene of action. Some of these vessels were more powerful than any which Admiral Dewey had in his fleet, and the German Admiral behaved in a way which came very near bringing on serious trouble between his country and the United States. Admiral Dewey's firmness put an end to the disagreeable attitude of the Germans, but he at the same time received assurances of support from Captain Chichester, in command of the English ships, which were of great value. This almost open act of friendliness, which recalled the old days in China when Commodore Tatnall went to the aid of the English, declaring that "blood was thicker than water," was merely representative of the attitude of the English Government. The sympathies of Europe were with Spain, but England stood by the United States, and this fact did more to wipe out the past and make the relations between the two countries what they should have been long before than all the years which had elapsed since the bitter days of the Civil War.

England's attitude, moreover, toward the United States during the war with Spain was only a part of the general policy of the Government then in control. When the Panama Canal, the interest in which had been steadily growing, reached a point where the United States was determined that the Canal should be built, it was found that the Clayton-Bulwer treaty was a

THE CHAMPION MASHER OF THE UNIVERSE
By Gillam in "Judge."

stumbling-block to any movement on the part of the United States. The American feeling was so strong that Congress was only too ready to abrogate the treaty by its own action, but, the question being brought to the attention of Lord Salisbury, the English Government showed itself more than willing to join with the United States in superseding the Clayton-Bulwer treaty by a new one under which the United States should have a free hand in dealing with the Canal. The first Hay-Pauncefote treaty failed, owing chiefly to its having incorporated in it a provision by which it was agreed that the Powers of Europe should be entitled to join in the neutralization of the Canal. This, on our part, was of course inviting the destruction of the Monroe Doctrine, and the Senate amended the treaty. England refused to accept the Senate amendments, but proceeded to make with us a second treaty which conformed to the changes proposed by the Senate, and this was ratified without opposition.

The policy manifested by the attitude of England in regard to the Canal question, which came soon after the end of the Spanish War, was closely followed, and was indeed enlarged, by Mr. Balfour when he succeeded Lord Salisbury as Prime Minister. President McKinley, in his desire to settle all possible outstanding questions with Great Britain — questions which related entirely to Canada — had brought about a meeting of an Anglo-American commission in Washington. It became evident that all questions could be easily arranged, with the exception of the Alaskan boundary, and upon that the difference was so sharp that the commission adjourned without having reached any conclusion at all in any direction. All the other differences remained in abeyance, but the Alaskan question became constantly more perilous. Nations, like men, will fight about the possession of land when they will fight about nothing else, and the Alaskan question, which caused a great deal of feeling in the Northwest, was rapidly approaching the dangerous stage. A treaty to submit the boundary of Alaska to an international tribunal, consisting of three Americans and three representatives of Canada and Great Britain, was made and ratified in 1903. The English representatives were two distinguished Canadians and Lord Alverstone, the Lord Chief Justice of England. The case was fully argued, and the decision was almost wholly in favor of the contention of the Unites States, which was owing to the action of Lord Alverstone, who decided in the main against the Canadian claim.

Thus the one question which was pregnant with real danger was eliminated, and the other questions with Canada were rapidly disposed of during the succeeding years of President Roosevelt's Administration while Mr. Root was Secretary of State. One treaty settled the international boundary, another provided for the protection of the fisheries on the Lakes, another for the international waterways, and, finally, the long-contested question of our rights in the Newfoundland fisheries went to The Hague for determination under a treaty framed by Mr. Root.

All these important agreements which made for the best relations between Great Britain and the United States grew out of the attitude of England at the time of the Spanish War, and were due to the policy of which Mr. Balfour in particular, and Lord Lansdowne, the Secretary of State for Foreign Affairs, were the chief exponents. In a speech at Manchester Mr. Balfour said:

"The time may come — nay, the time must come — when some statesman of authority, more fortunate even than President Monroe, will lay down the doctrine that between English-speaking peoples war is impossible."

To that sound policy Mr. Balfour and Lord Lansdowne strictly adhered, and to their action we owe both the settlement of all these differences with our northern neighbor, which have so perplexed us and, as a necessary consequence, the good relations which now exist between Great Britain and the United States, and which it is to be hoped will always continue. The policy might have been adopted in 1798 as well as in 1898, but Mr. Balfour and Lord Lansdowne were the first English statesmen who not only saw, but put into effect their belief, that the true policy for England was to be friends with the United States, and that friendship could be brought about by treating the United States, not as had been the practice in the past, but as one great nation should always be treated by another. They came to us, it is true, in the hour of our success, but none the less they are entitled to a place in the memory of Americans with Burke and Fox and Chatham, with Cobden and with Bright, who did not forget the common language and the common aspirations for freedom in the days when the Americans were a little people struggling to exist, or in those darker days when the government of the United States was trying to preserve the unity of the great nation which Washington had founded and which Lincoln was destined to save.

THE following pages contain advertisements of a few Macmillan publications on kindred subjects

A GREAT WORK INCREASED IN VALUE

The American Commonwealth

By JAMES BRYCE

New edition, thoroughly revised, with four new chapters

Two 8vo volumes, $4.00 net

"More emphatically than ever is it the most noteworthy treatise on our political and social system." — *The Dial.*

"The most sane and illuminating book that has been written on this country." — *Chicago Tribune.*

"What makes it extremely interesting is that it gives the matured views of Mr. Bryce after a closer study of American institutions for nearly the life of a generation." — *San Francisco Chronicle.*

"The work is practically new and more indispensable than ever." — *Boston Herald.*

"In its revised form, Mr. Bryce's noble and discerning book deserves to hold its preëminent place for at least twenty years more." — *Record-Herald*, Chicago, Ill.

"Mr. Bryce could scarcely have conferred on the American people a greater benefit than he has done in preparing the revised edition of his monumental and classic work, 'The American Commonwealth.'" — *Boston Globe.*

"If the writer of this review was to be compelled to reduce his library of Americana to five books, James Bryce's 'American Commonwealth' would be one of them." — *Evening Telegram*, Portland, Ore.

THE MACMILLAN COMPANY
Publishers   64–66 Fifth Avenue   New York

The Government of England

By A. LAWRENCE LOWELL

President of Harvard University; Formerly Professor of the Science of Government; Author of "Colonial Civil Service," etc.

In two volumes
Bound in the style of Bryce's "American Commonwealth"

New Edition.   Cloth, 8vo, $4.00 net

The New York *Sun* calls it: —

"The remarkable work which American readers, including even those who suppose themselves to be pretty well informed, will find indispensable . . .; it deserves an honored place in every public and private library in the American Republic." — M. W. H.

"Professor Lowell's book will be found by American readers to be the most complete and informing presentation of its subject that has ever fallen in their way. . . . There is no risk in saying that it is the most important and valuable study in government and politics which has been issued since James Bryce's 'American Commonwealth,' and perhaps also the greatest work of this character produced by an American scholar."
— *Philadelphia Public Ledger.*

"It is the crowning merit of the book that it is, like Mr. Bryce's, emphatically a readable work. It is not impossible that it will come to be recognized as the greatest work in this field that has ever been produced by an American scholar." — *Pittsburg Post.*

"The comprehensiveness and range of Mr. Lowell's work is one of the reasons for the unique place of his 'Government of England'— for its place in a class by itself, with no other books either by British or non-British authors to which it can be compared. Another reason is the insight, which characterizes it throughout, into the spirit in which Parliament and the other representative institutions of England are worked, and the accuracy which so generally characterizes definite statements; all contribute to make it of the highest permanent value to students of political science the world over." — EDWARD PORRITT in *The Forum.*

THE MACMILLAN COMPANY
Publishers   64-66 Fifth Avenue   **New York**

Historical Essays

By JAMES FORD RHODES, LL.D., D.LITT.

Author of "The History of the United States from the Compromise of 1850 to the Final Restoration of Home Rule at the South in 1877."

Cloth, gilt top, 8vo. Price, $2.25; by mail, $2.43

TABLE OF CONTENTS

I. **History.** — President's inaugural address, American Historical Association, Boston, December 27, 1899.
II. **Concerning the Writing of History.** — Address delivered at the meeting of the American Historical Association in Detroit, December, 1900.
III. **The Profession of Historian.** — Lecture read before the History Club of Harvard University, April 27, 1908, and at Yale, Columbia, and Western Reserve Universities.
IV. **Newspapers as Historical Sources.** — A paper read before the American Historical Association in Washington on December 29, 1908.
V. **Speech Prepared for the Commencement Dinner at Harvard University, June 26, 1901.**
VI. **Edward Gibbon.** — Lecture read at Harvard University, April 6, 1908.
VII. **Samuel Rawson Gardiner.** — A paper read before the Massachusetts Historical Society at the March meeting of 1902.
VIII. **William E. H. Lecky.** — A paper read before the Massachusetts Historical Society at the November meeting of 1903.
IX. **Sir Spencer Walpole.** — A paper read before the Massachusetts Historical Society at the November meeting of 1907.
X. **John Richard Green.** — Address at the gathering of Historians on June 5, 1909, to mark the placing of a tablet in the Inner Quadrangle of Jesus College, Oxford, to the memory of John Richard Green.
XI. **Edward L. Pierce.** — A paper read before the Massachusetts Historical Society at the October meeting of 1897.
XII. **Jacob D. Cox.** — A paper read before the Massachusetts Historical Society at the October meeting of 1900.
XIII. **Edward Gaylord Bourne.** — A paper read before the Massachusetts Historical Society at the March meeting of 1908.
XIV. **The Presidential Office.** — An Essay printed in *Scribner's Magazine* of February, 1903.
XV. **A Review of President Hayes's Administration.** — Address delivered at the Annual Meeting of the Graduate School of Arts and Sciences, Harvard University.
XVI. **Edwin Lawrence Godkin.** — Lecture read at Harvard University April 13, 1908.
XVII. **Who Burned Columbia?** — A paper read before the Massachusetts Historical Society at the November meeting of 1901.
XVIII. **A New Estimate of Cromwell.** — A paper read before the Massachusetts Historical Society at the January meeting of 1898.

"The author's grasp of detail is sure, his sense of proportion seldom, if ever, at fault, his judgment of a reader's interest in a subject admirable, and his impartiality can never be doubted. No one need hesitate to hail Mr. Rhodes as one of the great American historians." — *New York Sun.*

THE MACMILLAN COMPANY
Publishers   64-66 Fifth Avenue   **New York**

AN IMPORTANT BOOK

Lectures on the American Civil War

Delivered before the University of Oxford

By JAMES FORD RHODES, LL.D, D.Litt.

Author of "The History of the United States From the Compromise of 1850 to the Final Restoration of Home Rule at the South in 1877," "Historical Essays," etc.

Cloth, colored map, $1.50 net; postpaid, $1.62

These lectures, delivered before the University of Oxford in May, 1912, inaugurated a course on the History and Institutions of the United States. While written for an English audience, they are an attempt to relate concisely the antecedents and the salient events of our Civil War. Mr. Rhodes's deep conviction that the war was due to slavery is cogently set forth; his story of the decade before 1861 shows the resistless march of events toward the bloody consummation. The events of the war itself are grouped about Lincoln, Lee, and Grant, three heroes of undying interest; the assassination of Lincoln in his hour of success is the culmination of the tragedy.

"The fairness and clearness with which these lectures are written and the critical judgment which has reduced the number of details and made a unity of the war, give a merit to the book that places it in the front ranks of works on the Civil War." — *Boston Evening Transcript.*

"The lecturer's study of a war which marks an important epoch in modern civilization is an admirable piece of work." — *London Athenæum.*

"The author seems to us to be eminently fair in dealing with historic facts. The book is written in fine spirit and will be a welcome addition to the literature of the subject." — *New York Baptist Examiner.*

"From every point of view this is a study of exceptional quality." — *Washington (D.C.) Star.*

THE MACMILLAN COMPANY
Publishers   64-66 Fifth Avenue   New York